FOLLOWING
CAESAR

ALSO BY JOHN KEAHEY

Sicilian Splendors: Discovering the Secret Places
That Speak to the Heart

A Sweet and Glorious Land: Revisiting the Ionian Sea

Venice Against the Sea: A City Besieged

Seeking Sicily: A Cultural Journey
Through Myth and Reality in the Heart of the Mediterranean

Hidden Tuscany: Discovering Art, Culture, and Memories
in a Well-Known Region's Unknown Places

FOLLOWING
CAESAR

From Rome to Constantinople,
the Pathways That Planted
the Seeds of Empire

JOHN KEAHEY

ST. MARTIN'S
PRESS
NEW YORK

First published in the United States by St. Martin's Press, an imprint of
St. Martin's Publishing Group

FOLLOWING CAESAR. Copyright © 2023 by John Keahey. All rights reserved.
Printed in the United States of America. For information, address St. Martin's
Publishing Group, 120 Broadway, New York, NY 10271.

www.stmartins.com

Designed by Steven Seighman

Maps: Ken Gross, Millinocket, Maine

The Library of Congress Cataloging-in-Publication Data
is available upon request.

ISBN 978-1-250-79240-2 (hardcover)
ISBN 978-1-250-79241-9 (ebook)

Our books may be purchased in bulk for promotional, educational, or business
use. Please contact your local bookseller or the Macmillan Corporate and
Premium Sales Department at 1-800-221-7945, extension 5442, or by email
at MacmillanSpecialMarkets@macmillan.com.

First Edition: 2023

10 9 8 7 6 5 4 3 2 1

*For Professor Gerald L. (Jerry) Grotta,
the journalism professor who taught me
how to be a reporter, teaching lessons that
sustained me through newspapers and beyond*

CONTENTS

INTRODUCTION

Caesar: *Let me have men about me that are fat,*
Sleek-headed men, and such as sleep o'nights:
Yond Cassius has a lean and hungry look;
He thinks too much: such men are dangerous.
> —William Shakespeare, *Julius Caesar*

This was an eagerly awaited journey, designed to follow as closely as possible the ancient routes of three Roman roads: the Via Appia and the Via Traiana in Italy and the Via Egnatia across the Balkans and through four countries. I would follow several travelers, most prominently Julius Caesar on his way to wage war with his onetime son-in-law and lost friend, Pompey. This three-month-long journey had to be launched despite the reality that a pandemic was roaring its way around the globe. After a year's delay waiting for the proper vaccines and for key countries such as Italy and Greece to reopen after requiring all their citizens to isolate, the trip could finally be planned for the fall of 2021.

In crossing a handful of borders, eight Covid tests were required, some from pharmacies within two days of crossing, others at border stations performed by customs officials poking long-stemmed, cotton-tipped sticks through car windows. Paperwork had to be presented at each stop so officials could track me down if anyone I was around during these transits came down with the disease. It was unnerving knowing that despite two vaccinations and a booster, I could still get sick and be forcibly isolated, unable to travel to do my work. But the tests—some costing heavy fees, some free at a couple of borders—were always negative. Masks were worn everywhere, especially in Italy, and businesses were rigorous in checking this American's CDC proof of vaccination card. Only one uninformed restaurant worker, after I had visited dozens of such establishments over three months, refused to acknowledge the CDC card and turned me away. Fortunately, in the tiny village of Nemi, south of Rome, there was another restaurant nearby that understood the card was all that American travelers could have. And its food was excellent! We foreigners did not have access to the digital Green Pass system available to Italians.

These hurdles aside, the trip worked out well. With one major exception. Albania, which has a nice selection of preserved Via Egnatia segments, was open to travelers midpandemic during the beginning of this journey. In early November, the plan was to go by ferry with my Brindisi friend, Danny Vitale. He had offered to use his Italian-registered vehicle during a three-day visit since my French rental car was not allowed in that country. That mobility would allow us to visit the battlefield near Dyrrachium, today the port city of Durrës, where Pompey defeated Caesar and chased him into Greece. Then, in neighboring Greece at the Battle of Pharsalus, Caesar eventually destroyed his rival.

Our plan was to make our base in Elbasan, a city in the middle of this section of Albania. In Roman times, when the province was known as Illyricum, this city harbored a big way station, a "mansion," along the Via Egnatia that eventually grew into a rather sizable city. The drive across this west-east section—Durrës to the North Macedonian border—would take only three hours, so distances are short and easily doable in a series of day trips in the time we had set aside.

But the pandemic in that eastern Balkan nation grew, and our tickets were canceled. The ferry service let only commercial truckers on board. Commerce must still be allowed to flow, pandemic or not. Tourists—even working travelers—were blocked. Maybe it was a blessing. After three months of travel, I never tested positive in the handful of tests I took. Perhaps going to Albania would have been my downfall, and Danny and I would have been forced into isolation for ten days, a disaster for both our schedules.

For this book's purposes, I have chosen out of habit to use B.C. and A.D. for ancient dates. They correspond to BCE and CE used by other writers. For the three-month journey, I have told the story in a sequence starting in Rome and ending in Brindisi for the Via Appia. Then, I jumped across the Adriatic to North Macedonia, down into Greece, and on to Istanbul in Turkey. Many places were visited out of sequence. To keep things simple, I wrote about them as if they were taken in order. For example, I wrote about the Egnatia segments to Philippi that I had missed my first time through and then experienced on my return trip from Turkey. And I wrote about Sinuessa, Minturno, and Itri as I was returning to Rome. Discovery is the crucial element of a journey like this, and I would sometimes learn about places and their roles along the Via Appia and the Via Egnatia after I had passed through and was headed elsewhere. Such places were worth a return trip, and those visits became key elements in the story.

Last, I visited places near the Via Appia but not on it, places such as Bari on the Adriatic coast and Troia and Herdonia farther inland. These were towns and ruins on the Via Traiana, a road ordered built by Emperor Trajan three hundred years after the Via Appia. And I had longed to see the ancient ruins of Cannae, overlooking the plain where Hannibal handily defeated a massive Roman army. Since Hannibal had driven his Carthaginians along portions of the Via Appia in Southern Italy and is written about elsewhere, I felt Cannae was important.

And during a short drive away from the Via Appia, I visited the Golfo di Pozzuoli, where the towns of Bacoli, Baia, and Pozzuoli are located. Pozzuoli, known in ancient times as Puteoli, is where Saint Paul came ashore to face his Roman captors. This bay was a common spot where travelers, diplomats, and armies would disembark from ships and head, on secondary roads, to join the Via Appia at Capua or Sinuessa to begin a journey to either Rome or points southeast.

All these places are a cherished part in this story. But to keep the sequences in order, I tell their stories in the final chapter.

Of course, an undertaking of a book of this magnitude could not have been accomplished without a lot of help. I met most of these good folks while traveling, simply by asking a lodgings host if they knew someone who was an expert or who could help me solve a particular problem. Almost none of them were lined up in advance. They fell generously into place as I went from town to town and were eager and willing to help. It is a long list, and I wish I could describe in detail how each contributed.

I need to start with my wife, Connie Disney, who tolerates

my solo working travel and is always available for consoling and advice. She will occasionally meet up for a few weeks' stretch. But the pandemic threats kept her at home this time. I also need to recognize friends, both accomplished historians, who reviewed my manuscript to weed out any errors or to force me to control any speculations. They are Dr. Leonard Chiarelli of Salt Lake City, Utah, a leading authority on Muslims in Sicily who has helped me with more than one book, and Lou Mendola of Palermo, Sicily, who with his wife, Jacqueline Alio, are authorities on the Kingdom of Sicily that includes much of Southern Italy. The writings of these good folks were an invaluable part of my research.

And I am grateful to the website Poetry in Translation for granting permission to use its translations of the Roman poet Horace's *Satires* and the ancient writer Virgil's *Georgics*.

Others who helped:

EMILIANO BOMBARDIERI, Ariccia

FRANCESCA GNANI, Albano

STEFANO ACETELLI, Campagnano di Roma, guide for Rome segment of the Via Appia

ROBERTO D'OTTAVI, Terracina, host

SABINA MAGLIOCCO, University of British Columbia, folklorist

ANTONIO IANNIELLO, Santa Maria Capua Vetere, host

ANTONIO ROBERTO, San Nazzaro, host

ROBERTO PELLINO, San Giorgio del Sannio, guide

MARIA GRAZIE MAIONE, San Giorgio del Sannio, interpreter

DANNY VITALE, Brindisi, guide and friend

MARCO CAZZATO, Brindisi, B&B owner

CHRISTIAN NAPOLITANO, Muro Tenente, archaeologist

SONJA PENDIKOSKA, Ohrid, North Macedonia, host

VALENTINA GODOROSKA, the Via Egnatia south of Struga, North Macedonia, guide

VIKTOR BUSHINOSKI, Heraclea, North Macedonia, guide

GEORGIA DELIMPANIDOU AND GEORGE RAPTIS, Edessa, Greece, hosts

MAKIS KONIDIS, Edessa, Greece, amateur historian and pilot

HARIS TSOUGARIS, Archaeological Museum of Thessaloniki, Greece, archaeologist

ALEXANDROS LAMPRIANIDIS, Philippi, Greece, guide

SOULA TSOLAKI, Kavala, Greece, guide

LÜTFI BAYDAR, Turkey, guide

ANGELOFABIO ATTOLICO, Bari, author

NICO MOSCATELLI, Foggia, authority on Herdonia and the Via Traiana

THE FAMILY OF GENNARO OPERA; wife, Silvia Damiani; daughter, Anna Opera, Bacoli, for hospitality

ARIANNA CASTIGLIA, Bacoli, guide

GINO PEZZULLO, Piscina Mirabilis, Bacoli, guide

GENNARO RIPA, Minturno, the Via Appia, historian

MARGARET STENHOUSE, Ariccia, author of *The Goddess of the Lake*

MARIA GUNILLA, Nemi, B&B owner

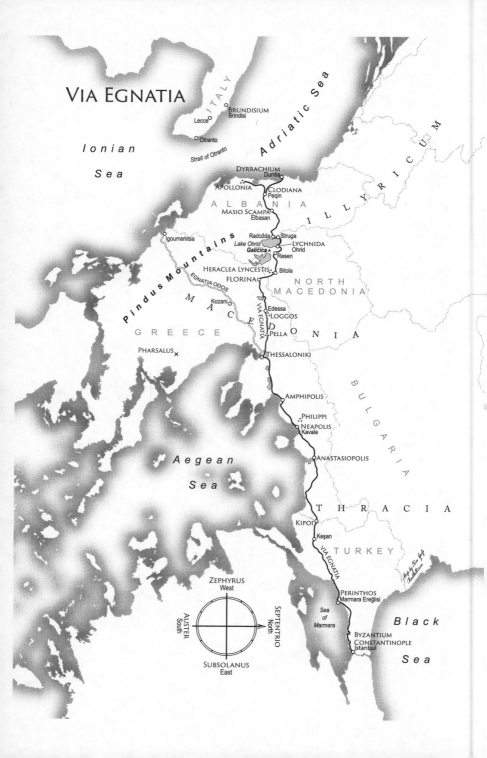

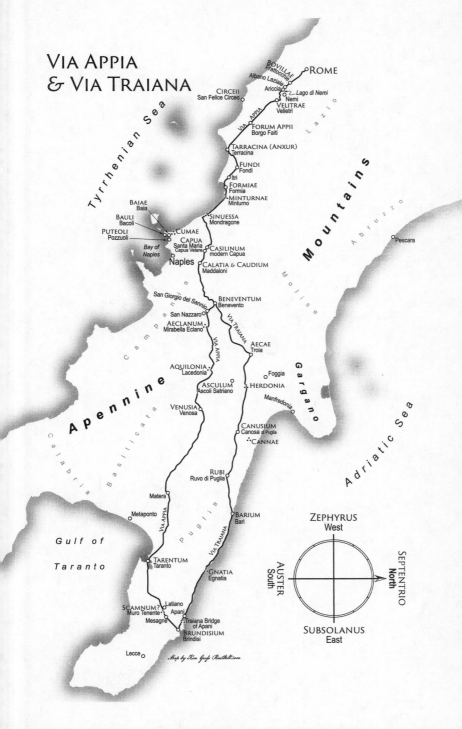

FOLLOWING
CAESAR

BORN OUT OF NECESSITY

Appia longarum teritur regina viarum.
Queen of long highways

—Roman poet Statius

I t begins like most things: there is a need or a sense of preservation or, simply put, cold ambition takes over and cannot be squelched. The people who became Romans, traditionally in the eighth century B.C., were first interested only in preserving their hilltops. Then, over a few hundred years, as their wooden and stone huts evolved into humble brick structures and then into columned superstructures, they climbed down those slopes, comingled with other nearby hilltop dwellers, and, after the rule of at least four kings, created a republic. From that republic's earliest years, Romans elected consuls who became military leaders and then began looking beyond their hill-lined valley with the Tiber River running through it. There were other people—some friendly and some not so—elsewhere in this hinterland beyond that famous river that was named after a mythical river-god of the earliest Romans, Tiberinus. This waterway, the second-longest on the Italian Peninsula, was a natural transportation route that also provided a line where foes squared off on opposite banks, battling for control of rudimentary bridges. To keep from being taken over, Romans had to build, over time, successive walls, ever expanding their city outward and absorbing those cross-river rivals. Eventually, early Roman soldiers—cobbled together in rough, barely organized gangs—needed to look beyond their river valley to protect their still-small city from interlopers.

The most critical threat, once the Latins absorbed neighboring Etruscans into their society and subdued local populations, was a people to the south and east known as Samnites, who occupied Italy's central highlands, which are now part of Italy's Campania region. For a half century, from 341 to 290 B.C., roughly more than two centuries before the birth of Julius Caesar, the Romans fought the Samnites and their allies in three wars.

The first war occurred when the people of Capua, located to the south and east of Rome, appealed to the Romans for help against these powerful invaders. The war ended in a treaty, and Capua was firmly under Roman banners. Then, Rome created colonies in Samnite territory, initiating a second war in which Romans lost critical battles before reversing their fortunes and securing another treaty. In this struggle, Rome learned valuable lessons in military organization and tactics from the well-armed Samnites. It adopted a warrior philosophy that served it through its republican years and well into the empire.

Of course, a third war was inevitable. A much-improved and better-disciplined Roman army defeated Samnites, Umbrians, and Etruscans in a battle in Central Italy, followed, in 291 B.C., by a Roman victory over the Samnites in Aquilonia, a town still using that ancient name, and established the colony of Venusia, today's Venosa, which figures later in our story. Again, a treaty. This time, Rome, still fated to fight other battles on the peninsula against a variety of different peoples in its efforts to unify Italy, emerged as a dominant player.

The Samnite wars are critical to understanding why Roman roads such as the Via Appia and the Via Egnatia to the east of the peninsula became so important in the thousand-year history of the republic turned empire. It was during this multilayered conflict that one of the earliest roads and certainly the most famous, the Via Appia, emerged. And while figuring mightily in defeating the Samnites, its success eventually spawned a series of roads all over Europe, North Africa, east to the Black Sea, and into the Middle East. And they all led to Rome.

Appius Claudius Caecus enters our story principally during the Second Samnite War. A writer and political leader, he had to put in time as a military tribune if he wanted to be elected consul. That conflict gave him such a moment. Can we imagine him perhaps ensconced in his tent near a potential battlefield wondering how a large army can make its way through a nearly roadless, muddy environment, hacking through forests, moving quickly with enough supplies to last it through a long march and major battles and to allow reserves to arrive in the nick of time?

No matter how the idea popped into his head, Appius saw the need for a mostly level, mostly straight road that allowed heavy traffic to move perhaps twenty-five miles a day. Such a road would be hewn from volcanic stones hard enough to keep armies, wagons, and horses out of the mud and to quickly meet and engage an enemy. Some Romans opposed it. They worried that the enemy could use such a road to do the same to them. But Appius, newly appointed censor beginning in 312 B.C., got its first segment built within five years and lived long enough to see it extended all the way to friendly Capua, some 130 miles from Rome, by 307 B.C.

It began somewhere near the entrance to the Roman Forum, across from the spot where the Colosseum was built a few hundred years later. The exact spot of its actual beginning could be beneath a nearby roundabout. An article in *National Geographic* reports that to discover its beginning, "the Ministry of Cultural Heritage has been digging out small, deep strips of pavement—so far, unsuccessfully."

At any rate, it moved from the Forum area, mostly in a straight line, to the faraway village of Anxur, now known as Terracina. From there, it shifted slightly inland to a place called Fondi, then headed back toward the coast passing through Itri, and, after a stretch along the Mediterranean, it turned southeastward to inland Capua. The name of Itri, a village that figures later in this story, could have been derived from the Latin word *iter*, which means "route" or "way," appropriate because the early Via Appia, its ancient stones covered by modern pavement, still flows through its historic center.

Within another half century, with the Samnites out of the picture, the Via Appia—referred to as Regina Viarum or Queen of Roads—was pushed to Beneventum, Venusia, Tarentum, and on to the port city of Brundisium, arriving there about 191 B.C. These places, with the Via Appia's stones still under modern roads, and often below farmers' fields, live on today as Benevento, Venosa, Taranto, and Brindisi.

Some researchers, studying how surveyors got the Via Appia so straight from south of Rome to Terracina, believe the ancients, by sighting on certain stars like the divine twins Castor and Pollux to lay out portions of the route, wanted to appease gods who were considered allies. Such a function would be important for a military made up of true believers. Real or not, the researchers have surveyed the route based on star alignments that were present in the skies above south-central

Italy two thousand years ago. Castor and Pollux do figure into it. It is up to conjecture whether the religious aspect was mentioned strictly to motivate Roman soldiers who, when not engaged in local battles but still being paid, would be charged with surveying, engineering, stone quarrying, and other hard, physical tasks. Slaves taken from conquered villages along the route could be used, but Roman soldiers did much of the work.

We moderns can imagine how this road looked from viewing photographs of one of the ancient sweeps open to public view. A popular section is a few miles south of the Roman Forum area where modern roads overlie the beginning of that ancient road. This section is preserved in the Parco Regionale dell'Appia Antica, an archaeological park of nearly eighty-five hundred acres and ten miles long. Within it are preserved stretches of original stones glistening in the sunlight with shadows of leaves dancing across their basalt surfaces. That's the way the road started out in the time of Appius, pushing through the gate of Rome's early defensive Servian Wall; later another gate for the Aurelian Wall was built over the route.

The writer A. J. Langguth paints a lovely description of the original road's composition as it made its way to Capua under Appius's direction: "Near Rome itself, Appius built the road with blocks of gray basalt, but as it wound past cypress and pine trees and across the Pontine marshes, his road became only gravel and, at its farther points, it was no more than a dirt footpath amid weeds and flowers."

The road, of course, was improved over the decades and most principally a few centuries later by the emperor Trajan, who adjusted its route here and there. Those volcanic stones were supplemented by large, hardened slabs from local quarries cut out of nearby hills. At Anxur/Terracina, for example, the original road steeply ascended a high promontory where the Temple of Jupiter Anxur still dominates the skyline. This routing, which extended toward Fondi a few miles away, ignored the original concept of a straight, level highway. But Trajan's engineers figured out a way to bring its course back down to level ground and resume its southeastwardly run toward Capua. They made room for it by cutting back a high, massive stone wall at the sea's edge.

Near this Campanian city, now with the modern name of Santa Maria Capua Vetere, the Via Appia met up with a slightly earlier Roman road, the Via Latina. It doesn't have the fame of its bigger, slightly younger sister; modern highways don't follow much of its route, although a modern portion of a rail line between Rome and Naples is built over a stretch. While it was not built to Appius Claudius Caecus's high standards, it likely was improved over time. But the Via Appia, a quicker course from Rome to ancient Capua, was preferred.

Today, the route is generally followed by Italy's highway Strada Statale 7, or SS7. It is generally known as Via Appia Nuova (new) when it closely parallels this ancient road's route. It appears on maps and road signs simply either as Via Appia or with "Antica" tacked on when modern pavements cover the same alignment as the ancient Roman road.

Another road that captures our interest, the Via Egnatia, was begun in 145 B.C., nearly 170 years after the start of the Via Appia. It, too, was built to high Roman standards. It originally ran from the ancient Illyricum port of Dyrrachium, now modern Durrës in Albania, through the southwest corner of North Macedonia to Thessaloniki in Greece and farther east to Philippi. Eventually, it was pushed all the way to Byzantium, which later was named Constantinople in honor of Constantine the Great. We know it as Istanbul.

Over the centuries, the Via Egnatia provided a route for armies marching back and forth across the Balkan Peninsula. During the Roman era, Saint Paul and his companion Saint Silas, in ca. A.D. 50, traveled along the route between their landing at Neapolis, now the Greek city of Kavala, to the ancient city of Philippi where he preached. The two eventually followed the Via Egnatia to Thessaloniki, where Paul left the road and was spirited to Athens for his protection from angry Thessalonian Jews who objected to him preaching in their synagogue.

Eventually, accompanied by Saint Luke, he would sail to Italy, coming ashore at Puteoli, now modern Pozzuoli. He and his party followed local pathways for a few miles up to the Via Appia, likely joining it near the ancient village of Sinuessa, and followed it to Rome where legend says Saint Paul was eventually beheaded. Silas's fate is not known, but he was evidently spared, as was the chronicler Luke.

The Via Egnatia—sometimes left to fall into disrepair, other times wonderfully maintained—was ruled over by a number of Balkan-based powers, principally the Eastern Roman Empire that emerged when the Roman Empire was divided into west and east in A.D. 395. It also was known as the Byzantine Empire, which lasted until 1453, when Constantinople fell to the Ottoman Empire.

Saint Paul aside, for centuries, pilgrims from Europe followed the Via Egnatia to Constantinople and then traveled across the Bosphorus Strait to the Holy Land on other Roman roads. Today, modern travelers can journey along much of the ancient Egnatia's nearly 700-mile original length, almost double the 360-mile-long Appia, from the Adriatic coastline to where the ancient road ended a few dozen feet from Istanbul's mosque, the Hagia Sophia.

And any discussion of these two roads that connect Rome to the eastern edge of its empire must include Emperor Trajan's great building feat, the Via Traiana. It was begun in A.D. 109 and, leaving the Via Appia at Benevento, it followed a southeastward route to the coastal city of Bari, and then down the coast to Brindisi. Ironically, the Via Traiana between Benevento and Brindisi is two miles longer at 205 miles compared to the 203 miles of the Via Appia through the interior. The Via Appia, despite its reputation for running straight and level, has numerous hills and other difficult terrain to cross south of Benevento to as far as Venosa. Taking Trajan's mostly flat coastal route saved travelers a day. With traditional Roman roadbuilding ingenuity, the Via Traiana tied together earlier footpaths that were mostly level and ran close to the sea. It ran southeast to Bari, turned south, and connected with the Via Appia just outside of Brindisi's walls.

Today, archaeologists know that at the height of empire, some twenty-nine roads led out of Rome. The Via Appia and its predecessor by just a few decades, the Via Latina, were just the beginning. An engineering website, Interesting Engineering, reports that 372 roads connected the empire's 113 provinces. These provinces extended from Britain to Mesopotamia in the Middle East and from the Danube River to Spain and North Africa. These paved roads, built primarily for military reasons, covered fifty thousand miles.

What kinds of ancient building techniques kept these roads and dozens of others like them functioning around the inland sea known as the Mediterranean for more than two thousand years? After all, this incredible roadbuilding process continued for more than seven hundred republican and empire years. And they continued to serve shifting populations, other empires that came and went, and different governments for centuries beyond.

Their heavily engineered construction was, of course, a marvel. We can look at stylized drawings that show the various layers of road design and assume that this was consistent in nearly all Roman roadbuilding. It wasn't. For example, Roman road pavements depended on the kind of stone that was available in each local area. Builders certainly could not transport to farther-flung sites a massive volume of surface stone like that used immediately south of Rome's historic center. Also, high groundwater levels and swamps in some segments might mean the trenches holding the different layers would not need to be as deep as they might elsewhere or that they would require more maintenance as the decades passed.

This said, the process of building the Via Appia and other roads in favorable terrain generally involved digging a trench twenty to twenty-three feet wide—wide enough for legions with men marching six abreast—and up to six and a half feet deep, or at least until bedrock could be reached. A lime mortar would line this trench to even out imperfections, and rocks small enough to be hand carried would cover this substructure. On top of these, a more gravel-like layer of stones would be spread to facilitate water drainage. And above that, to a depth of nearly a foot toward the road's edges and nearly one and a half feet in the middle, gravel, coarse sand, or earthen fragments and lime mortar would be spread. Did the creation of this middle hump, which was often higher in very wet areas and obviously used to send rainwater tumbling to the sides and into stone-lined drainage channels, give rise to the English term "highway"? Finally, pavement stones would be laid, many cut to fit snugly against their neighbors.

Researchers tell us that miniature bridges were placed over small streams and paved fords provided passage over shallow spots in rivers. Wider rivers, some of which two thousand years later are mere trickles, were spanned by wooden bridges that eventually were replaced by great stone bridges. Evidence exists in foundations and broken arches. A few are still used by modern traffic and farm machinery in isolated rural areas.

One researcher writes that unavoidable marshes and swamps were traversed by wooden pontoons, and bridges were built atop those structures. And sometimes, water-carrying viaducts acted as long bridges. All this work created structures and roadways that lasted for centuries. And it told potential rebellious upstarts that Roman legions could arrive quickly. That knowledge was often sufficient to keep the peace.

One other aspect of this building process, in addition to running through existing villages, was the creation along the routes of new settlements and major military camps. Inns were established for travelers either on foot or on horseback.

Maps clearly show the routes of these ancient roads through the modern world of Southern Italy and the Balkans. Some brief sections are well established and preserved, allowing the visitor a quick glance or a hiker a pleasant journey over stones that have been trod upon for centuries. Other sections are hidden three or four feet below modern roads. Still others are buried below farmers' fields or covered over by modern homes and businesses. Historians and archaeologists can only speculate where they are.

These roads call out to be seen and followed, at least as far as knowledge and weather allow. Towns and villages that still exist were created as way stations to serve armies, travelers, pilgrims, and dispatch riders who, carrying messages from the empire's distant corners to emperors, needed fresh horses every twenty or thirty miles. And many no longer exist except in our imagination, sheltered in protected archaeological sites that among piles of stones and fallen columns can only hint at a magnificent past. There is "the then and the now" that must be seen and absorbed. It's a journey of more than 1,000 modern miles—or 1,070 Roman miles—and it must begin in Rome and end in Istanbul.

2

A BEGINNING

Leaving great Rome for Aricia, a modest inn
Received me: the rhetorician Heliodorus
Was with me, most learned of Greeks: to Forum Appii,
Then, crammed with bargemen and stingy innkeepers. We
Took this lazily in two days, though keener travellers
Than us take only one: the Appian's easier taken slow!
                                                    —Roman poet Horace

I n the early fall of 2021, as the poet Horace did roughly 2,060 years before, I left "great Rome" for Aricia, today's Ariccia, a mere twenty miles distant, following as closely as possible his route, known today as the Strada Statale 7, or SS7. He knew the stones beneath his feet only as the Via Appia, which, beginning in 312 B.C., was hammered across wide plains, chiseled through valleys, cut through deep woods, and built up along the muddy edges of marshes almost three hundred years before his journey, likely undertaken sometime between 40 and 37 B.C. He doesn't go into much detail about why he was making the journey, but history tells us it was part of a diplomatic mission ordered by Octavian, the future emperor

Augustus, to help mend his tenuous political relationship with his former co-ruler Mark Antony.

With a diverse assortment of friends and fellow diplomats, Horace traveled along the Via Appia's well-laid-out route, leaving it at Beneventum where his party turned eastward and followed a rough collection of undeveloped and soggy footpaths to the Adriatic coast. At the tiny fishing village of Barium, they headed south toward their destination, the port city of Brundisium in southeast Italy.

More than a century later, under the emperor Trajan, this muddy divergence from the Via Appia would be remade into the Via Traiana. Historians differ in judging the time it took travelers to make this Rome-Beneventum-Barium-Brundisium journey; best guesses range from thirteen to seventeen days. They did it on foot, riding in carts, and on horseback. The mostly level divergence eastward to the coast would have saved the exhausted travelers one or two days. This route avoided the rolling hills found along the traditional Via Appia passage from Beneventum south to Horace's birthplace of Venusia, and then turned eastward at Tarentum on the inside of Italy's heel.

Why did Horace write about this journey? And for which meeting between Octavian's and Antony's negotiators was the journey undertaken? Historians disagree, and we can only speculate. Today, Horace's Fifth Satire is likely viewed as a work of fiction, based loosely perhaps on a real journey at some point between 40 and 37 B.C. Some, including the eighteenth-century historian Edward Gibbon, believe he intentionally treated lightly a trip of such diplomatic importance "to convince his enemies that his thoughts and occupations on the road were far from being of a serious or political nature." After all, Horace was a poet not a historian like Livy or Tacitus.

The various negotiations that resulted in at least two major treaties followed a love-hate relationship between Julius Caesar's grandnephew and designated heir, Octavian, and Octavian's close ally Antony. The pair had teamed up to defeat, in 42 B.C., Caesar's murderers, Brutus and Cassius, at Philippi in Northern Greece. They already, a year earlier, had divided the then-vast Roman Republic into three parts, much like Caesar had done decades earlier with his future enemy Pompey and the general who had defeated Spartacus, Crassus. Following Caesar's murder, Octavian and Antony, along with the lesser-known Roman general Marcus Aemilius Lepidus, carved up the soon-to-become empire: Octavian controlled the empire's west, Antony took over the east, and Lepidus was handed North Africa. Octavian eventually shoved aside Lepidus, who was exiled to Circeii (modern Circeo), a prominent mountain on the Tyrrhenian coast south of Rome.

This left just Octavian and Antony to squabble. Originally, in 40 B.C., in a gesture of continued goodwill, the Treaty of Brundisium included the marriage of Octavian's sister, Octavia, to Antony. (Likewise, Antony, a few years later, handed over his stepdaughter Claudia to become Octavian's bride in what reportedly was a short, unconsummated marriage.)

Was Horace at the signing of that first pact? Probably not, historians conclude. Over the next few years, Antony and Octavian still were having problems working together to rule the future empire. Each was ambitious and jealous of the other. At the time of the first treaty, Octavian was twenty-three; Antony was forty-three and had fought with and been loyal to Caesar through numerous campaigns beginning in 55 B.C., when Octavian was only eight. He felt the republic belonged to him, not this young upstart. Despite this, and because they together had defeated Caesar's murderers at Philippi just two years earlier, both men attempted accommodation, at least temporarily. So the pact was followed in 37 B.C. with the Treaty of Tarentum. This attempt to recement relationships was pushed by the sister/wife Octavia, resulting in another reconciliation of the two powerful men. Of course, we know that it all fell apart anyway. Antony was famously involved with Cleopatra in Egypt, and a new war was inevitable. The two men clashed in 31 B.C. at Actium, off the western coast of Greece. Octavian won decisively. Antony and Cleopatra returned to Egypt and, the following year, committed suicide twenty days apart. Octavian, now unchallenged, was named Rome's first emperor in 27 B.C., assuming the title Augustus.

Today's pleasant, friendly Ariccia appears to show no trace of its former glory as a significant Roman center along the vitally important Via Appia. It is a footnote important only to ancient history and only piqued my curiosity because Atia Balba, the mother of the man who became Rome's first emperor, grew up there. She was the daughter of Julius Caesar's younger sister Julia Minor, making her son Caesar's grandnephew. Octavian's father, Gaius Octavius, who grew up along the Via Appia eight miles away in Velletri, viewed a marriage to a niece of Julius Caesar as a pathway to fame and fortune. It worked for him. An effective general, he eventually became the governor of the eastern Roman province of Macedonia and was on track to become a consul of Rome before his untimely death in 59 B.C.

The ancient highway did not climb the hill Ariccia is built on and around but rather ran through the lower village, likely the site of Horace's "modest inn" that he shared for one night with his travel companion, the rhetorician Heliodorus. Nothing of this ancient town remains, and a road sign appropriately identifies the roadway around the bottom of the hill as Via Appia Antica. This original road continues across a wide valley and through a heavy wood, which must have been tough going for Appia's builders.

It reconnects with the modern Via Appia, the SS7, near Octavian's father's birthplace of Velletri, south of Ariccia. From here, the Via Appia continues southward, the modern pavement perhaps as much as six feet atop the ancient stones. It stretches along that famous straight line through now-nonexistent Forum Appii, the second day's destination for Horace and his fellow travelers, to the coastal town of Terracina thirty-four miles away.

The modern center of Ariccia is atop one of the Alban Hills, where more than two thousand years ago, a Roman forum likely stood in all its colonnaded glory. From medieval times to the present, the busy town gradually expanded downward along this high ground's flanks, spreading once again, as in Roman times and earlier, around the bottom. Ariccia was besieged by various armies over the centuries following the fall of empire. Finally, the Arabic Saracens destroyed it in 827, and its surviving citizens abandoned the ruins on the hill's lower flanks and moved up to the ancient acropolis, founding a new community.

Ariccia was my first stop of what was to be a three-month journey along the ancient roads that tied the city of Rome to Byzantium long before the Roman Empire replaced the republic. I arrived at midday, planning a stay of five days. The forty-five-minute trip from Rome was along the combined route of the new and ancient Via Appia through an area of the Lazio region known as Castelli Romani, a significant center for wine production in the Colli Albani, or Alban Hills. The ancient route, newly paved and full of traffic, split off the SS7 a short distance north of the town, leaving me to drive up to the hill-top center that sits warm and inviting with buildings yellowed by time.

Here is the likely spot where the ancient forum long ago sprawled across the hill's level top and later, after the Saracen destruction, where the survivors refounded their new center. It is a large square with open spaces dotted by outdoor tables for a restaurant, a bakery, and a bar, all full of locals enjoying their midday break in the warm Italian sun.

Along the piazza's south edge, a narrow shop-lined village street that bumps into the Via Appia Nuova dips down and connects to the Via Appia Antica far below. At the north edge, a tall stone-and-brick bridge that was built at the order of Pope Pius IX in the 1850s, destroyed by retreating Germans in World War II, and then rebuilt in 1947 and again in the late 1960s spans the valley crossed by the ancient road far below.

The piazza is flanked by buildings dating back to the six-teenth and seventeenth centuries, including a baroque church designed by Gian Lorenzo Bernini, the designer of the piazza at Saint Peter's Basilica in Rome. On the opposite side of the square is the Palazzo Chigi, which was built in the sixteenth century by Ariccia's first landed owners, the Savellis, and later dramatically remodeled in the baroque style under Berni-ni's direction in the seventeenth century, when the town was passed on to the Chigis. It now houses the village's municipal offices and, at the back, opens to comfortable gardens.

Late in the morning of my first day of travel after landing in Rome, I drive south across the hilltop square, the center of

Ariccia and likely site of the now-gone Roman forum from antiquity. My in-car navigator is taking me to the first B&B of my three-month journey, a small studio owned by Emiliano Bombardieri. I pass the front of Bernini's church, and the Via Appia Nuova pushes me straight ahead down the short hillside at the south edge where I turn off and find myself on the Via Appia Antica. The good feeling of being on that road, which would have been in Horace's footsteps, ends quickly as the navigator takes me around the edge of the town's hill onto another road a few hundred feet from the massive stone-and-brick bridge. The B&B address has a house number that does not show up on any of the buildings, despite the navigator telling me that I have arrived. I stop, get out, and wander around looking for the correct numbers.

Some men in a fenced-in area are operating machinery in what appears to be a car repair shop. I holler, getting their attention above the noise. "Salve. Qualcuno conosce Emiliano?" (Hello. Does anyone know Emiliano?) Before they could answer, an upper window flies open. A woman shouts down, pointing to the building next to where I was parked. "Sì. Dall'altra parte della strada." (Across the street.) He is at work, she says. I knew I was early. The website said check-in was 4:00 P.M., and I was here in the early afternoon. She shouts down his phone number. Since I was so early, I decide to wait awhile and unwind from the drive. There's a bench next to Emiliano's house. But within a few minutes he drives up; the lady across the street had called him. We greet each other and he takes me to my quarters in a small separate structure behind his two-story house. The gate is iron and old, bursts of rust showing here and there, but it is functional. The path through a small garden with a table and chairs lead to an unpainted wooden walkway with wobbly slats leading to the small structure that, when Emiliano opened the door, showed a comfortable interior. It was a pleasant room with a worktable, double bed, and up a short step, a more-than-adequate bathroom with a good-size shower, rare for the kind of rentals I usually seek.

I asked my new host, as I usually do on fact-finding trips, if he knew anyone who was knowledgeable about the Via Appia. "I don't know, immediately," he said in excellent English. "Let me ask around." A few hours later, after I had finished an excellent lunch of pasta carbonara (my favorite Roman dish) in the village center, he texted me the name and number of a woman in the next village to the north, Albano, just a mile or two along the Via Appia Nuova. I called her, and Francesca Gnani agreed to meet me that evening for coffee.

We met in a small square just off the Appia and walked to a bar with outdoor seating. It was getting dark and under trees and umbrellas with tea and coffee knocking back the chill of the early September evening, we talked about the Roman road and my plan to follow its length and the length of its extension, the Via Egnatia, to Istanbul.

First, I told her, I wanted to speak to someone familiar with the history who could meet me at the beginning of the roadway at the southern edge of metropolitan Rome. She had a name for me. Stefano Acetelli. "He speaks good English I am told, and he is a good tour guide who knows his subject well. He is willing to meet you."

So, it was all arranged and by people I had met less than a few hours before. My practice of asking for help, advice, and recommendations while traveling over these many years paid off again. Before we parted, I mentioned that I needed to find a camera shop to replace a broken lens cap. "Let's get it on Amazon," she said. I thought it would take too long I told her, knowing that the fastest I could get something at my home in the

United States was a few days or even longer. "I will order it now," she said, whipping out her phone. "It will be delivered to my house tomorrow morning. Come by on your way to Rome." She had it ordered within two minutes and charged to her account. I paid her in cash.

The next morning, I went by her home, a beautiful stone structure that had long been in her family and was located on a wide tract of land in an open area outside of Albano. She handed me a small Amazon box. The cap was there, and it fit beautifully. We had tea and good conversation. "Tell me how it goes with Stefano," she said. "Is he a friend?" I asked. "No. When Emiliano called me, I called around. Someone recommended Stefano to me."

The next morning, I drove north, back toward Rome, again following the Via Appia along the original route now part of SS7. Just north of Ariccia sits Frattocchie, a small village near the south end of the narrow, ten-mile-long Parco Regionale dell'Appia Antica, where the original protected route in its final couple of miles devolves into a dirt track, devoid of surface stones and rough on cars.

I was told at one point not to consider driving on it without a four-wheel-drive vehicle. I followed that advice, driving only to the section's south end and gazing northward along the slash of original road. It was near here that Tiberius, in A.D. 14, ordered a circus built, reportedly in honor of Augustus, who died that same year. A scattering of mausoleum ruins also lay about nearby. This section of modern Frattocchie was known in ancient Roman times as Bovillae. It was the first village that the Via Appia initially reached south of Rome when construction started in 312 B.C. Here, the park ends, and the ancient route weaves in and out of the modern SS7 southward through Ariccia and beyond.

Today, Frattocchie is a destination for folks starting their walks or bicycle rides from the park's beginning in Rome. Seeing the ancient route that way, one can experience it while treading on original stones and wandering among the remains of dozens of monuments, big and small.

My memory is often fragile, but I recalled that perhaps twenty years earlier a friend and I drove from the Appia's beginning through what is now the park all the way to the pavement's end just north of Frattocchie. I knew then that American soldiers, in 1944, rolled along this stretch of Via Appia Antica to liberate Rome from the Germans. Today, cars are banned for much of that distance, but in the late 1990s we passed all the monuments, mausoleums, and remains of stone houses the Romans had built along their Queen of Roads. Also then, we saw women, spaced out along the road's stone surface, leaning against or sitting on ruins along the edges, waiting for someone to stop. This disturbed us, especially my Italian American traveling companion. Now, twenty years later, they have moved elsewhere.

I am quite early for my meeting with Stefano Acetelli at the beginning of the Via Appia Antica on Rome's south edge. I park opposite the tall, imposing Tomb of Cecilia Metella and the Castrum Caetani, two of the best-known and most photographed structures near where the park begins. The day is cloudy with occasional sprinkles. Whatever sun breaks through the muddy sky overhead is muted and flat. Occasionally, I spot blue above me, the light rain stops, and, knowing I have more than an hour before Stefano arrives, I wander up the ancient road, finding the spot where the first preserved section of the roadstones begins. They are wet, but even in the occasional darkness that sweeps across the sky, they glisten. The surface, far from level like a modern highway, shows stony humps cut into narrow ruts from bygone wheels and separated by gravel-filled cracks. It must have been hard walking for soldiers wearing sandals—burdened with heavy armor and weapons. I had read somewhere that the stone-covered via was for supply carts, wagons, and men on horseback. Soldiers, I read, often marched in formation on either side, hence the origin of the word "sidewalk." True? If so, like "highway" the Romans gave us equivalent Latin words for our modern vocabulary. Today's rough surface along this stretch of the Via Appia can't have been helped when the American army—nipping at the heels of the Germans fleeing north in June 1944—rolled its heavy tanks and other armored vehicles over it en route to the center of Rome.

Walkers and people on bicycles rented at a shop attached to a coffee bar that sits on the edge of the bumpy, irregular via are moving along, heading south. I walk, finding the roadway and its stones uncomfortable. There's an uneven dirt path on either side, but a walker is regularly forced to move over for passing bicycles. In this portion of the park, uninspiring stone structures, some no taller than I am, mark the spots where mausoleums once held the remains of noble Romans, or perhaps some are simply the remains of stone bases that held statues of white-robed emperors or generals honored for long-ago battles.

I walked for perhaps a mile, passing occasional ruins without any clear identities attached as well as small brick remnants of structures identified as the Tomb of the Servilii and the Tomb of Seneca. The Servilii were members of a family of ancient Rome; the tomb was used for fewer than two centuries before it slowly, imperceptibly began to decay. A carved relief showing three heads of a son, father, and mother was long ago removed and now rests in the Vatican Museums. Seneca's *sepolcro* is often referred to as "so-called" given that authorities are uncertain of its naming origins and even whether the Spanish-born Seneca (1 B.C.–A.D. 65), who was one of Rome's greatest rhetoricians and philosophers, was ever buried there. This is typical of many ancient tombs, some of which are named for well-known individuals who never were interred within.

Weeks later, for example, I would visit a tomb farther south along the ancient Via Appia that is identified as belonging to the great Roman lawyer, politician, and general Cicero. No one believes Cicero's remains are anywhere near there. I often wonder where the bodies of famous Romans truly ended up unless they were cremated, as was Julius Caesar's. I expect many were unceremoniously dumped into the Tiber River after assassination, or maybe a few made it into a proper burial in still-undiscovered tombs far below modern streets and buildings.

Perhaps many empty tombs are named for individuals just to serve as a reminder to posterity that they existed. In Seneca's case, he was forced to commit suicide because he allegedly plotted against his former student Nero. Would he get a proper burial? And Mark Antony ordered the murder of Cicero, who despite well-documented service to the Roman Republic early in his career, was known for loyalties that shifted more often than a barometer in springtime. He had survived throughout the various civil wars that marked the republic's dying days at the hands of unabashedly ambitious winners like Caesar, Octavian, and Antony, not to mention the losers in those struggles: Pompey, Brutus, and Cassius. Pompey, we know, had an ugly death in Egypt, losing his head to Egyptians eager to please

Caesar. Brutus and Cassius died by falling on their swords on the plain of Philippi; their bones likely long ago plowed under by succeeding generations of farmers. No tombs for any of these men.

Stefano arrives just as I walk back to our meeting point. We get acquainted, and he tells me about the structures a few hundred yards north of where we're parked. On the east side of the ancient road is a wide-open space with a series of ruined structures that still hint at how they must have looked two thousand years earlier. This is the Circus of Maxentius and, nearby, the restored Mausoleum of Romulus.

Stefano and I talk about Constantine, the grantor of respectability to early Christians, who allowed this area to survive despite Maxentius being his great enemy. He was a usurper emperor who challenged Constantine in various spots around the empire, their battles culminating in A.D. 312 near Rome. Constantine said he had seen, high in the sky, a religious symbol—the superimposed Greek letters *c* and *p* for chi and rho—associated with Christianity.

Believing that the vision meant he would win the battle, he ordered his soldiers to paint the symbol on their shields before engaging the army of Maxentius. Constantine won, of course, and became the first emperor to allow the once-persecuted Christians to practice and grow their faith in what had long been a pagan world.

Maxentius, long before this confrontation took place, had ruled in Constantine's absence, beginning in A.D. 306. At the point where we now walked along the ancient road, just a few hundred feet north of the Tomb of Cecilia Metella, he had built, in the early years of the fourth century, a tribute to his son, Valerius Romulus, bearer of the same name as Rome's mythical founder nearly a thousand years earlier. Sources differ. One told me that Romulus died at age four and another said he was a teenager, but both agree that A.D. 306–312 is the date of the mausoleum and the circus's construction.

Maxentius had his son deified as a god, and the mausoleum could also have been a final resting place for family members. Maxentius didn't make it into the round structure in this open plain now sweltering in Rome's early September heat and punctuated here and there with a handful of tourists. With Constantine on his tail, he tried to escape on his horse across the Tiber on a temporary bridge of boats, the Milvian Bridge, and tumbled into the river. His body was recovered, he was decapitated, and his head was carried through the streets.

Maxentius had many wonderful things built in his son's circus. Created out of concrete, tuff blocks, and bricks and offering a wide, oblong track for racing chariots, it could perhaps hold ten thousand people. Again, in tribute to his son, the emperor had placed the Obelisk of Domitian, covered in hieroglyphs, in its center. It had broken into five pieces—in some forgotten battle or perhaps during a small earthquake?—and was buried over the centuries. Then, at the order of Pope Innocent X in 1649, the pieces were carried to Rome where the artist Bernini restored them and placed the dazzling, four-sided spire atop the Fontana dei Quattro Fiumi in the Piazza Navona.

We walked the short distance back to our meeting point. Waiting was a sky full of water, ready to burst over us. It did, and we climbed into my car where we sat, as rain pounded us, for nearly two hours in deep discussion about this section of the Via Appia. Stefano taught me a lot, not only about Maxentius and his deified son but also about the Tomb of Cecilia

Metella and the construction of this beginning section of the Via Appia.

We're near a road known as Via Appio Pignatelli, which joins the Appia Antica on its left side and then curves south a few miles to where it joins the modern Appia Nuova. At its juncture with the ancient road are remains of tombs, probably built in the empire's dying days. Other much smaller roads connect as well; these are pilgrims' routes past the numerous churches in this part of the park. In fact, less than a mile from the Via Appia's beginning at the Roman Forum is the Chiesa San Cesareo de Appia. This is significant because from the Forum to this point, the Via Appia was built over the top of the earlier Via Latina, and here they branch off from one another. The Via Latina, built in roughly 334 B.C., just twenty-two years before construction on the Appia began, headed in a southeasterly direction out of Rome and along the Alban Hills, well to the east of its more famous sister. The two roads merge once again near ancient Capua. Today, the Via Latina branch is known for a short distance on modern Roman street maps as the Via di Porta Latina. It runs past the magnificent Basilica of Saint John at the Latin Gate, built in the late fifth century A.D., and then turns into Via Latina on its way out of the modern metropolitan area. This asphalt road in places shows the occasional ruin alongside and dives in and out of Rome's suburbs, but it does not garner even close to the attention granted to the Via Appia.

Stefano, I discover, is well educated in the ancient and medieval history of this part of Italy. He is the perfect kind of tour guide a traveler wants, one who knows his subject and does not guess at answers when his client asks off-the-wall questions. We spent a lot of time at the Tomb of Cecilia Metella, which is one of the more dramatic structures along the Via Appia—

and certainly one of the most photographed. This area features rustic structures and farmhouses on either side of the road as well as the empty stone framework of long-deconsecrated churches. An inscription on the side of the tall, circular tomb tells us that Cecelia Metella was the wife of Crassus, who likely was the oldest son of the Roman general Marcus Licinius Crassus. The elder Crassus was a close ally of Caesar's, and he is the man who ultimately defeated, in 71 B.C., the slave Spartacus who led a rebellion. Crassus's army captured six thousand surviving members of the slave army. He had crucified them along the Via Appia, one after another, past the spot where his daughter-in-law's tomb now stands, to Capua, some 132 miles away. Her tomb wasn't built until sometime between 30 and 20 B.C. We know almost nothing about her life, so we can only speculate whether she or Crassus's son ever witnessed the spectacle of the long rows of dying men.

Stefano told me that archaeologists have not fully explored the interior of the drumlike sepulture. It has changed somewhat over the centuries, with certain features added and others taken away. It sits in a slightly elevated position, giving it and the area around it a commanding view of the countryside. It evolved into a fortress in the eleventh century, and a fortified village was created around it. In the fourteenth century, a *palazzetto* that became known as the Castrum Caetani was built next to Cecilia's tomb. And again, over the centuries, ownership changed hands numerous times, from one wealthy family to another. Then, in 1589, Pope Sixtus V wanted to tear down the tomb and use its stones in new construction elsewhere. Cooler heads prevailed, and his plan was canceled. The tomb in all its structural glory had indeed become symbolic of its place along this ancient road beloved by all Romans.

Stefano, in a quick aside, happened to mention that this

section of the Via Appia Antica, for perhaps no longer than a half mile or so, was constructed differently than elsewhere along its long route to Brundisium. Here, under that brief stretch, is the tail end of a prehistoric lava flow—dating back perhaps 160,000 years—that had been caused by an eruption of a volcano more than twelve miles to the south. With a petrified lava stream underneath, builders did not have to dig as deep to give the road a firm base for the gravel and stones on top. All interesting and I thought a rare bit of information not generally found in the books and articles I consulted in learning about the road's history.

It wasn't until I put two and two together and discovered that the lava that had helped create this durable, indestructible road base came from a volcano that carved out a giant lake-filled crater and became the scene of one of Rome's most enduring myths and the site of a Roman emperor's pleasure retreat. Coincidentally, I would be there the next day, wandering the shore of the beautiful, sky-blue Lake Nemi, searching for the Roman goddess Diana the Huntress.

3

GODDESSES AND DESPOTS

*The temple is in a sacred grove, and in front of it is a lake
which resembles an open sea, and round about it in a circle
lies an unbroken and very high mountain-brow,
which encloses both the temple and the water
in a place that is hollow and deep.*

— Greek geographer/historian Strabo

*And to see what at last? The lakes of Albano
and Nemi: a pair of spectacles
slung over that great nose with the tip upwards,
which is Monte Cavo . . . and then
the summit of the mountain remained
as if exiled from the world.*

— Sicilian author Luigi Pirandello, "Pallottoline," from
the collection *La giara*

Nemi, the village and the lake, are a few miles southeast of Ariccia and just off the Via Appia Antica. The
massive crater, composed of dark-colored igneous
rock known as scoria, surrounds the deep lake and provides

a beautiful vantage point high above for fewer than two thousand residents. It was choked long, long ago by dark, dense beech, oak, and chestnut forests. The volcano, before falling into a deep slumber ten thousand years ago, had dramatically rearranged the prehistoric landscape, shaped the Alban Hills, and sent rivulets of lava at least twenty miles north. One of those rivulets stopped short of where Rome would rise millennia later and ended up under a stubby section of where the Via Appia would begin.

Lake Nemi is a crater lake, fed in prehistoric and ancient times by tumbling waterfalls. The village is much newer, rising around a castle in the ninth century A.D.

In Roman times, this area along the edges of the lake was frequented by wealthy Romans who, seeking to escape the stifling, odorous city in summer, built country estates. Overgrown ruins of some of those estates still exist. The historian Suetonius wrote during the imperial era of the early Roman Empire that Julius Caesar, when he was Pontifex Maximus, or chief priest and head of the state clergy at around age thirty-seven, "having laid the foundations of a country house on his estate at Nemi and finished it at great cost, he tore it all down because it did not suit him in every particular, although at the time he was still poor and heavily in debt."

It seems that Rome's future dictator was quite fond of elegance and luxury in his young adulthood. Suetonius writes that Caesar's armies "carried tessellated and mosaic floors about with him on his campaigns." Later in his military career, he was granted several triumphs, highly stylized military parades through Rome for many of those successful campaigns, but some sources say he also was granted an "ovation," a lesser triumph, for some unknown victory.

This smaller parade took place at Nemi along a route

known as the Via Sacra, created in the earliest of Roman times and perhaps even before the Romans dominated these nearby peoples who had lived here for many centuries and who eventually evolved into a loose federation known as the Latin League. One source says this pathway was "rebuilt with basalt stones under the reign of the fifth king of Rome, Lucius Tarquinius Priscus." This legendary king is thought to have ruled Rome from 616 to 578 B.C. For him to have *rebuilt* the Via Sacra suggests that its creation is lost to the mists of forgotten time, perhaps as far back as the twelfth century B.C. It was used by those Latin peoples who regularly traveled to the mountaintop to honor the supreme god at the Tempio di Giove Latiaris. When the Romans arrived, this god became Roman Jupiter. According to historical sources, his temple was the center of the Latin League's religious and political life.

A short distance down the mountain was the Temple of Diana Aricina or Nemorensis, or Diana of the Sacred Wood or Diana the Huntress. The people of the Latin League—and later the Romans—worshiped her there as the protector of hunting and fishing, patron of childbirth, and the divinity of the underworld.

The Via Sacra ran up the slopes above Lake Nemi and, during the ovation, took Caesar and his soldiers past Diana's temple just above the lake's shoreline to the summit of the extinct volcano, where the ancient cult of *Iuppiter Latiaris* worshiped their major deity, Jupiter. Diana and Jupiter had been merged into Roman culture from the Greek gods Artemis and Zeus. Historians Lou Mendola and Jacqueline Alio tell us, "The society of ancient Rome never made the slightest pretense to deny that its predominant cultural precursor was Greece, embellished by some contributions from a few other civilizations, such as those of the Etruscans and even the Phoenicians."

The road, today a mere path, still exists in some spots, along with remnants of *crepidines*, ancient curbs made of peperino stone, a light gray or brown volcanic tuff infused with specks of basalt. What is left of this route, up Monte Cavo's steep slopes and through its thickset woods, is popular with modern hikers. This original section is part of a nearly sixteen-mile-long newly crafted loop, beginning and ending in the village of Nemi. It was created for hikers and bicyclists, and it swings back and forth along various hillsides.

The early people of this area, the members of the Latin League, were eventually overtaken by ambitious Rome, and these Romans continued for centuries to frequent the sacred woods and those two temples. Eventually, a temple to Jupiter was built in Rome's Forum, overshadowing the one atop Monte Cavo. It floundered on that mountaintop for centuries. During the Middle Ages, a hermitage dedicated to Saint Peter was built over Jupiter's temple site. In the late eighteenth century, temple stones were taken and used to restore a monastery that replaced the hermitage.

The goddess Diana continued to be honored long after Jupiter fell out of favor, probably until the fourth century A.D., and was eventually abandoned with Christianity's rise across the Roman world. Much of Diana's temple, but not all, was used as a quarry for construction material. Remains exist of it by the lake; Jupiter's temple is gone, replaced by a slew of television antennas and communication towers.

Caesar was not the only Roman to enjoy the idyllic slopes of Monte Cavo with the lake far below. His contemporary Cicero had a villa farther to the north of Nemi, on the northern edge of the volcano's outer crater rim and nearer the summit where Jupiter's temple dominated. It was at the ancient village of Tusculum, whose ruins are part of the modern town of Frascati, a place famous for its wines. Cicero fought to preserve the Roman Republic while Caesar, seeking to become dictator for life, seemed to be taking it toward empire. An orator, statesman, lawyer, scholar, and philosopher, Cicero is thought to have owned at least nine villas throughout Southern Italy, and ancient historians quote him as saying that the one at Tusculum was his favorite.

He fell into and out of favor with Caesar, often supporting the general's enemies, but Caesar welcomed him back into his arms at the southeastern port city of Brundisium. Cicero had briefly led a legion on the side of Caesar's enemy, Pompey, during one of the many civil wars through the first century B.C. After Pompey's defeat and escape to Thessaloniki in Greece, Cicero met the victorious Caesar on the Via Appia, just outside Brundisium. The two men dismounted and walked side by side at the head of Caesar's army.

Biographer Adrian Goldsworthy tells us that "the nervous orator was relieved and gratified by the warmth of his [Caesar's] greeting, which was followed by an immediate pardon and encouragement to return to Rome." Caesar's murder fewer than three years later and Cicero's lack of respect for Mark Antony eventually led to the famed orator's unceremonious end.

During my two visits to Nemi at the beginning and the end of my journey—along the Appia, Traiana, and Egnatia—I doubted that I would find any stones belonging to Caesar's estate. If he had that structure demolished, as Suetonius reported, someone else would have claimed the spot. I am not sure anyone today knows where it—or even Cicero's villa higher up on the mountain—might be located. My questions, about this and other ancient traditions surrounding the lake and village, drew mostly deep shrugs from folks in Nemi. *"Non lo so"* (I don't know) was something I heard often while exploring the mysteries of the place.

Much of the area around the lake today is built up with homes or covered in strawberry fields, olive groves, flower farms, horse pastures, and small vineyards, many surrounded by stone walls. Survivors of some of the ancient forests that once swept around this crater, casting dark shadows over its deep waters, are found here and there. Trails and narrow pathways abound. I walked along several, feeling the coolness of trees and their dark-colored oak leaves, punctuated here and there by giants whose ages might be counted in the hundreds of years.

During my second visit and with my three-month journey behind me, I regretted not attempting the Via Sacra to the top of Monte Cavo. I wasn't inclined to walk uphill to greet towers and antennas. That was a shortsighted decision. I passed up a chance to walk on stones laid down nearly three thousand years ago and nearly a thousand years before the ancient Via Appia was created. But time was limited. I wanted to spend whatever I had left to find the remaining stones and partial columns of Diana's temple. Mythology has always intrigued me, and I knew that Diana was the Roman version of the Greek goddess Artemis.

I had read that a Greek-turned-Roman goddess who had founded Ariccia, the site of my first stay during my Italian journey, had a temple just above the lake's modern shoreline.

At first, learning about her and visiting her temple was my only goal. My interest in Caesar's and Cicero's time there came with further study after I arrived. Diana's lake can truly be imagined as the "Mirror of Diana" when first seen. It is small and gives a sense of deepness, the kind that hides many mysteries.

The Roman emperor Caligula, in A.D. 41, spent time partying on huge boats he had built and launched on these deepblue waters. He was murdered a year later and his boats were sunk, but his time on Nemi must have been over-the-top. Did he visit Diana's temple, then just a few dozen feet above the lake's shoreline? Probably. Even emperors of Caligula's ilk still revered Roman gods and goddesses—at least publicly.

Myth, of course, has no roots buried deep in actual, known history. People needed a device to explain things about which they had no historical memory and certainly no scientific knowledge. Who did the early Romans think founded their city, which became a republic and then an empire? In addition to the legend of Romulus and Remus, they needed the writer Virgil to give them answers, even if they bordered on myth. He was ordered by Augustus to write what became the *Aeneid,* Rome's foundation myth. It was Rome's answer to the founding myth of Athens in Greece. The sea god Poseidon competed with Athena to be the patron of Athens. The winner was Athena, goddess of wisdom and war, who was born fully armed by leaping out of the head of Zeus. She offered the first olive tree, something that would give Athenians food, oil, and wood. All Poseidon could give the people was salt water to drink.

Ariccia, known to ancients as Aricia, was always there; no one truly knew of its origins. So, it had to have been the work of the goddess whose temple is an easy horseback ride or a short walk away in the woods above a nearby lake. After all, legend, as described by British poet and Greek myth authority Robert Graves, says that when Diana—under her Greek name Artemis—was only three years old, she sat on the knee of her father, the Greek god of gods, Zeus, and he gave her "not one, but thirty cities, and a share in many others, both on the mainland and in the archipelago; and I appoint you guardian of their roads and harbors."

Aricia then can be considered as one of her thirty cities, or at least one in which she had a share. The Greek geographer Strabo, visiting it during the late years of the Roman Republic, describes it this way:

> After Mt. Albanus comes Aricia, a city on the Appian Way; it is one hundred and sixty stadia distant from Rome. Aricia lies in a hollow, but for all that it has a naturally strong citadel. Above Aricia lies, first, on the right hand side of the Appian Way, Lanuvium [Lanuvio], a city of the Romans, from which both the sea and Antium [Anzio] are visible, and, secondly, to the left of the Way as you go up from Aricia, [is] the Artemisium [Temple of Artemis/Diana].

During my travels I came across many sites where temples to Diana had once stood. She often had different extensions on her name in many different places. At Nemi, it is the Temple of Diana Nemorense. In Formis, a tiny municipality just off the Via Appia at Santa Maria Capua Vetere—the town that was ancient Capua in Roman times—is the Basilica of Sant'Angelo. It once was referred to as *ad arcum Dianae* (near the Arch of Diana). This is because the eleventh-century sanctuary was built atop an earlier church that had been built on top of the Temple of Diana Tifatina. That appellation comes from Monte

Tifata, on whose western slope the basilica sits. The mountain's summit once held a temple to Jupiter, Diana's father. The slope above and to the side of the church had been burned over in some range fire that must have erupted a few months before my visit, sparing the basilica, the tiny village, and the wonderful Borgo Antico Ristorante, whose menu was full of dazzling local cuisine.

My friend, Dr. Sabina Magliocco, a University of British Columbia folklorist, put it in perspective. "The thing to know about the Greek and Roman gods and goddesses is that just like the Virgin Mary, they exist in different versions, everywhere localized," she told me in correspondence between Nemi and Vancouver, British Columbia. "As you observed, there isn't one Diana, as we are led to believe when we read Ovid or study the classics; there are an infinite number of Dianas, each linked to a place in the landscape and associated with different stories and symbols.

"This can indeed be very confusing, as when you have an allegedly virgin (read "single" and "independent") goddess like Diana shown as a mother figure. But what we need to keep in mind is that the version of Roman religion that was communicated by the classical authors is an official, elite one. [The] deities combined and recombined with local spirits tied to the land and families. Each had their own story, which differed from official versions."

Christianity, with its own stories to tell of faith and salvation, dressed up many of those myths to make its message more palatable to pagan peoples. Examples abound. One that I was curious about is Diana's Festival of Torches, the Nemoralia, which ran for three days around Lake Nemi, from August 13 to 15. Under Christianity, August 15 is the day of the Assumption of the Blessed Virgin Mary honoring the Savior's mother's ascension into Heaven. It would have been easy for early Christians to tie the Assumption of Mary to Diana. Diana, despite having no children of her own, was a mother figure, as was Mary, and one of Diana's responsibilities was protecting childbirth.

One of the earliest Roman historians, Cato the Elder, wrote midway through the second century B.C. about how Diana was celebrated during the "Ides of August." Emperor Augustus renamed it Feriae Augusti in 18 B.C. These ancient celebrations involved nighttime processions of torches and candles along Lake Nemi's shoreline and likely up the pathways through Diana's temple.

During my walk searching for that temple, I discovered clues that the pagan festival is even honored in modern times. Stapled to trees along a tiny country road were photographs showing torches punctuating the darkness. Nearly twenty-five hundred years later, it appears that modern people still honor the goddess who had so many tasks assigned to her by a loving father. Looking at the photographs, I had no idea how close I was to the temple ruins. The road I followed and where I saw the postings is a few hundred feet upslope. The woods are so deep that the remaining wall and broken columns cannot easily be seen. It took a second visit three months later—and directions offered by my host—to get me there.

My first visit to Nemi was less than a day long. I drove into the tiny village on a Saturday. It was crowded with late-summer tourists, and parking spots were almost nonexistent. I parked perhaps a half mile along the approach road just off the Via Appia Antica and walked into the place and its single main road bordered by small shops.

Nemi is a tourist town, with more coffee shops and restaurants than most Italian towns of its size. I stopped for a coffee and asked the young woman behind the counter how to get to the Temple of Diana. She pointed down that street to an arch that led to an overlook for the lake and said, "That way. That's all I know." I walked to the arch and peered at the valley below. The street turned sharply toward another smaller arch. There appeared to be signs suggesting cars could go no farther.

I went back into the heart of the village, found a place for a good Italian lunch, and read for a few hours while sitting at another overlook to the lake. Eventually, I walked back to my car and plugged in the words "Temple of Diana" into its navigator. The map led me around the lake for a few miles and up a road where I eventually found a small, weather-beaten sign with an arrow that proclaimed TEMPIO DI DIANA. I proceeded on foot up a steep trail wide enough for a small vehicle, sweeping past a field with a stage at one end and bales of straw set up before it as seating. Obviously, this was some sort of a concert venue that was finished for the season.

There was a narrow, ankle-deep grass-covered turnoff with a sign that simply said PARKING, but the main trail moved higher and curved around. This is where I saw the photographs of the torchlight processions. But there was no temple in sight, and there were no other signs. It was getting late. Heading back down, I met a German couple who told me they also were looking for the temple and had given up. We walked back to our cars. Obviously, it seemed that local officials did not want people to easily find the temple ruins. The woods, in early evening, were dark. I drove back to my lodging in Ariccia, figuring I would return in a few months and try again.

I returned to Nemi in late November, its days still moderately warm, the nights chilly. This trip would end in less than a week after my three-month rove along my Roman roads' itinerary. I would spend three days there, determined to find the sanctuary of Woodland Diana and hopefully get a sense of what the ancients must have felt in such an environment. Margaret Stenhouse, whose book *The Goddess of the Lake: Origins of a Myth and the Roman Ships of Nemi* is the best volume on the subject that I encountered. She writes that the natural combination of lake, woods, and extinct volcano:

> created an environment which inspired awe and reverence. It is easy to imagine that only a god could dwell in such surroundings, and that only the power of a god could dominate such a place. . . . It is whispered that the old Nature cult of Diana still lives on and in certain days of the latter part of the year, when the leaves turn yellow and glow with a burnished lustre in the soft, autumnal sunshine, every tree in the crater suddenly bears a golden bough.

My base in Nemi was a small apartment up a side street. Parking along the street's edge—the cars aligned in long single file—was packed. A car at the top would have to wait for a car coming up from the bottom before heading downhill. Complicating matters was the presence of larger construction vehicles whose crews were working on a structure adjacent to the building where I was headed.

I managed to make it to the front of my apartment where the owner, Maria Gunilla, was waiting in an open window high up on the first floor. Signs to the front and side warned me that no parking was allowed. Maria came down, helped with luggage, and was full of suggestions about where to seek a parking spot. As luck would have it, I headed downhill a few minutes later and a car along the side of the steep roadway pulled out ahead of me. I slid into the vacant spot and decided that's where the car would sit for the next three days. Nemi is small, and I assumed I would find a trail to Diana's temple through the forest just over the hill and down the slope toward the lake.

The next morning, Maria rose to the occasion with a text offering detailed directions:

"It is easy to go down on the beautiful path in the wood; not so easy to go up again. It is very steep." She instructed me to go through the arch at the castle where a small road traveled along a hillside with a wonderful view of the slope and the lake beyond. "Then after a smaller arch, hold to the left and that's the path. When you come to a sign, SPECO DI SAN MICHELE, go to the right." Within a hundred meters, she said, I would begin to see the walls of the temple ruins.

It wasn't quite that easy. After coming down the steep dirt and stone-strewn path, I turned right onto a road leading past various homes and farms, took another right turn, and found I was in the exact spot I had been three months earlier when I drove my car around the lake. Ouch. How do I go from here? There was the tiny, weathered sign I had seen then, TEMPIO DI DIANA, pointing up the same attenuated uphill road where I had seen the photographs of the August torchlight wanderings that groups of modern pagans had posted on tree trunks.

After just a minute or so of my frustrated mutterings, a young man, probably in his twenties, came down the little road. I stopped him. "*Come posso trovare il Tempio di Diana?*" (How do I find the Temple of Diana), I asked in my halting Italian. "Ah, you walk up this road," he said in perfect English, "and where you see the sign that says PARKING you turn in and walk several meters. You will see it on the right." I could have hugged him, but I didn't. I had walked past that parking turn twice three months earlier. We waved goodbye, and he said, "You will enjoy."

I almost ran up the steep, narrow road, turned left through the parking entrance, and walked through tall grass still damp with dew. I looked right. There was an ancient Roman wall behind a tall wire fence. There was no way in from this direction.

The heavily grown over parking area continued with the markings of what could be a trail with a fence on my left. I saw a woman working on the fence, which seemed to be her private property line. Behind her was a horse arena and a couple of young people riding horses. It appeared to be a riding school. I asked her if it was possible to get into the temple grounds, which now were surrounded by tall fencing. "No problem," she said, pointing to a spot farther along where a couple of men were working on a newly constructed two-story stone building. "That will be the center for visitors."

I walked onto the property where the men were working. A sign said CHIUSO (closed). I walked in; the men ignored me. Near the back of the new building was the edge of the exposed temple ruins. There was a small gate at the fence, unlocked. The site, while accessible, was supposed to be closed. Maria had told me it was problematic because it was so difficult for people to find, and there had been no development in recent years to make it attractive to visitors. She later told me that the new stone building would accommodate visitors when the site finally opened, and there would be improved access. There was a road that served the riding school, and that allowed workers to bring in heavy equipment and materials. But when? Anybody's guess, she said. But the reality of a beautiful new building nearing completion offers hope.

I walked through the gate and onto a long, grassy stretch of earth. On my left, buttressed up a steep hill, were ruins of what likely were small rooms in the temple. Farther along, there was an open courtyard area that once must have been roofed over. In the middle were four partial columns, just a few feet high. Beyond those was a long, beautiful wall, its surface a mass of stone squares placed in a diagonal design I have seen in several ruins around Italy and Sicily. And in the corner of the open courtyard there was a stone altar-like table with all sorts of offerings: a large potted anthurium plant with leaves beginning to shrivel in the fall weather; a couple of contemporary pots; various food items, such as small apples beginning to turn brown and unshelled nuts; small votives of various animallike figurines; a photo of a child; and various notes written, I assume, to Diana.

All this on the altar was a bit of modernity, items placed there by today's visitors honoring the goddess and perhaps asking her for help. There were no photos attached to trees in this area of the exposed ruins. I spent a couple of hours wandering back and forth and relaxing on ancient stones, warmed by the fading fall sunlight. I left this tiny compound, closing the gate behind me.

A few feet away, a small grove of olive trees badly in need of pruning looked inviting. In years of travel throughout Southern Italy and Sicily I seek out olive groves, admiring the gnarled trunks of the older trees. Here in their midst sat a white plastic chair. I walked over and plopped down, sitting there for perhaps another hour looking at the trees and, occasionally, glancing over at the wire fence and the ancient stone walls beyond.

I had been traveling for three months, and my mind wandered to the places I had seen at the beginning, starting with Diana's village, Ariccia, just a few miles away from her temple and her lake. At my trip's beginning, I had headed south from Ariccia to a point where the Via Appia began to run straight as an arrow in a Roman archer's quiver, all the way to the coast to another Temple of Jupiter high above Terracina. It was a route beautifully described by the poet Horace millennia before it became a modern Italian highway that runs just as straight over the top of its predecessor and through a grand canopy of Italian stone pines. This stretch had really marked the beginning of my journey.

Diana's exposed ruins could be walked around in perhaps fewer than five minutes. The site is small, contained. Archaeologists estimate that the original temple site millennia ago was enormous, perhaps extending over forty-five thousand square meters (more than eleven acres). What we can see is just a fragment of that kind of space. It would go well beyond the area around the new stone building as well as the nearby riding school and the few acres of olive groves around one edge.

I walked back to the bottom of the hill and the steep trail that my host Maria said would not be so easy going up. She was right. It was slippery dirt strewn with small rocks that promised at minimum a twisted ankle. And it was steep. Fortunately, every fifty feet or so I found a place to sit and catch my breath. What took me fifteen minutes to come down, took forty-five minutes to go up. I reached the top near the small arch that led into the village of Nemi. From there, I scanned the valley below and spotted the horse property and the adjacent remains of Diana's temple. What took two trips three months apart to this small village to find had been, from the beginning, in my line of vision. Hopefully, the authorities building that handsome stone welcome building will find a way to show future visitors how to get there.

4

HITTING THE ROAD

Roman roads brought unification to all peoples . . .
entwined under a single name—Romans. They were
world citizens who shared a common law. All were
Roman citizens, peers in their world . . . whether
they lived in Africa or in Hither Asia or on the
banks of the Rhine River. All looked to Rome.
                    —American explorer Victor W. von Hagen

I t appears that Horace spent only one night in what was then called Aricia before moving on with his travel companion, Heliodorus the rhetorician, to a tiny way station known as Forum Appii, or the Market of Appius, likely named for the builder of the Via Appia's first section, Rome to Capua. This place, or the memory of "place" since it is long gone, is midway along the famously straight portion of the Via Appia beginning south of Rome to Terracina. Today, that section begins a few miles south of Ariccia. Tourists speeding along it, flanked on both sides by magnificent Italian stone pines with their high umbrella tops, know it well. But if we consult an ancient map, found in *Barrington Atlas of the Greek and Roman World,* we discover that the Via Appia was rigorously straight to Terracina all the way from its beginning at the edge of Rome's Forum. Today the modern road is still mostly straight to Terracina, except for a few twists and turns through the Alban Hills.

One ideal early morning, in barely breaking light and sparse traffic, I put Ariccia behind me and, after a few miles, pulled over to the side of this famous road. My chosen spot of repose was at the beginning of the straight section just outside of Velletri, a hilltop town dating from prehistory and overtaken by Romans when Rome was ruled by kings. Historic battles were fought here in the eighteenth and nineteenth centuries, and in 1944 the Allies and the Germans were locked head-to-head in fierce fighting around where I was sitting comfortably and in peace. From here, at a point where the road slopes downward along Velletri's hillside, I could see the long sweep of the Pontine Marshes. This once-marshy scape edges down in a wide quadrangle between the sea and the foothills of the Aurunci Mountains a few miles east all the way to Terracina. It had been a land of soggy, mosquito-ridden marshes that troubled travelers, including the poet/diplomat Horace, and bedeviled Via Appia builders. The Greek geographer Strabo, who was Horace's contemporary, described the area our poet and his friends were experiencing firsthand as "marshy and sickly." It lasted, unfarmable and nonproductive, from ancient times to the early twentieth century. Mussolini had the marshes drained and resettled, between 1927 and 1939, into three thousand farms, eighteen villages, and five new towns.

Angelofabio Attolico, a friend from Bari (a port city on the Adriatic coast), is a major figure in an organization dedicated to preserving the route of the Via Francigena, which sometimes is directly on, or parallel to, the Via Appia. He drew my attention to the pathway for pilgrims heading through Italy to Bari or Brindisi and then across the Adriatic to transit the southern Balkans to Constantinople and beyond. The Via Francigena originated in the eighth or ninth century with a beginning in Canterbury, England (requiring, of course, a boat journey across the channel). I had once walked along a short portion in the area around Pietrasanta in western Tuscany. It was summer, and the trail—designed and paved for people or bicycles only or sometimes along local roads—was clearly marked and packed with hikers from across Europe. One man told me he had started in Canterbury and hoped, over two seasons, to make it to Jerusalem, avoiding war-torn Syria. I have often thought about him, and I wonder if he made it.

From where I'm sitting, the Via Francigena had departed from the Appian Way and was moved a short distance to the east along those foothills. The reason? Angelofabio said it was to get far away from the Pontine Marshes, which made travel in the Christian era difficult and unhealthy.

As I dug into my *caffè doppio* (double espresso) and *cornetto con crema* (cream-filled roll), picked up from a bar in Ariccia, I looked through a sheaf of notes and came across an entry about Julius Caesar. He, of course, traveled along this road many times. As a young man, before his fame put him in distinguished company, he—alone or with a companion— would have ridden past where I sat munching on a cream-filled croissant.

During his midthirties—at a time in his life when in the words of one biographer he "was still not all that important"—he worked hard to ingratiate himself with powerful men. One such powerhouse was the former consul Pompey, a highly popular general and winner of several triumphs through Rome for important victories. Caesar caught the attention of Rome's leaders and got the job as curator of the Via Appia in 66 B.C.

This was the perfect appointment. Biographer Adrian Goldsworthy writes, "Another way in which Caesar sought to woo
the electorate was by lavish expenditure." He "spent a good
deal of his own money to pay for the renovations and improvements he had made to the road and its associated structures."
This endeared him to townspeople along the route from Rome
to Brundisium and to travelers heading to Rome. As they journeyed along improved stretches of the republic's most important road, Caesar wagered that they would know what he had
done for them.

Apparently, his largess, which depleted a lot of his family
money, worked. He was elected in 65 B.C., at age thirty-five, to
a post of *curule aedile.* He and his fellow aediles were charged
with the maintenance and upkeep of the city of Rome and
the running of the fifteen-day Roman Games. Caesar had to
scrounge more money to make them spectacular.

His spending as curator of the Via Appia and then as aedile
put him deeply in debt to creditors who obviously felt he had a
bright political future. He didn't disappoint them, becoming a
highly successful general who subdued lands far beyond Rome
and bringing them—and their wealth—under the banner of
the eagle. One of those creditors was likely the wealthiest Roman of them all, Crassus, the general who defeated Spartacus
and who crucified six thousand of Spartacus's followers along
this very road, from Rome to Capua. I shudder as I look along
the stretch before me.

Years later, with Caesar's popularity and civic responsibilities growing and after becoming one of the greatest of Rome's
generals, he led armies up and down portions of this road to
go against his former hero Pompey in one of Rome's civil wars,
fought at the Via Appia's terminus, Brundisium, and across
the Adriatic in what today we call the Balkan Peninsula.

I would come across Caesar again, in Brundisium. For now, I was looking to find Forum Appii and see if any of it still existed. Before the day would end, I would also realize I was on the same route as another famous man from the earliest years of Christianity, the missionary Saint Paul of Tarsus, who passed along this same avenue to Rome and his martyrdom.

Forum Appii's location is described as near the beginning of a long, river-fed canal, the Decennovian, that runs parallel to the roadway all the way to Terracina where the Via Appia meets the sea. Terracina is roughly eighteen miles south, by today's measurements, from my parking spot. The canal, parallel to the road itself, still exists and denotes the eastern edge of what used to be the Pontine Marshes. And on this long section south of Ariccia to Terracina, the modern Via Appia, SS7, glides directly over the ancient roadway, effectively preserving the Roman-placed stones that are hidden well beneath the asphalt, as do modern cobblestone streets in many of the towns and villages the Appia Antica passed through.

Still wrapped in my thoughts, I headed south. The drive was short and pleasant. I had zipped along this section several years before on my way from Rome to Anzio to visit an American World War II cemetery. In those days, I had no idea of the road's historical significance, and the sign or two that I saw indicating it was the route of the ancient roadway had no real meaning. Now, shuttling more slowly beneath the plethora of umbrella-like pines and just a few feet above where sandaled Roman soldiers trod and emperors and generals rode, I slowed down, swallowing the scene whole.

Eventually, my car's navigator told me I was where Forum

Appii was supposed to be. The name is apparently still on some maps, but there is no archaeological dig going on anywhere near here, and there is no historical site identified for the ancient way station for travelers and canal boatmen. Forum Appii has disappeared. Its remains, except for two stone structures alongside the road, are hidden below the tiny village of Borgo Faiti. Some ancient tombs and the ruins of a bridge, known as Arches of San Lidano, are nearby.

One of the stone structures closely associated with Forum Appii stands perhaps ten feet tall and likely was part of something much larger. It has been identified as part of a memorial to Nerva and Traiano. Emperor Nerva was Trajan's predecessor, serving only two years, A.D. 96 to 98. "Traiano" is Latin for Trajan. He served from A.D. 98 to 117. A second, similar small tower of stone is dedicated only to Trajan.

Some four miles of the road was repaired under the direction of the two emperors, and two bridges, one at Forum Appii itself, were repaired. In addition to the partial monuments, only a scattering of relics from antiquity can be found here, along with traces of minor buildings and numerous fragments of decorative materials. At the edge of the roadway, there is also a Roman mile marker, number 43. Much of Forum Appii was still around in the eighteenth century when Pope Pius VI ordered that a post office be built when the road, then starting to be known as Via Appia Nuova, was rebuilt. Borgo Faiti, the village that was created over this spot in the 1930s when the marshes were drained, has only six hundred residents. And, yes, it has a post office.

As a visitor to Rome in earlier years, I had been duly impressed by the monuments still standing in honor of this emperor: Trajan's Column and the large ruins of Trajan's Market and Forum. Later in my journey, I would come across even more examples of what Romans accomplished under his nineteen-year leadership in the early second century.

But for the moment, the precise location of Forum Appii will remain a mystery. I knew from extensive reading that Cicero visited here and mentioned the place in correspondence with friends. Even Pliny the Elder got in the picture of this place. He wrote about the "Setino" wine, coming from the slopes of the mountains above Forum Appii. I also read a reference by Suetonius, a Roman historian who wrote a century after Horace, who said a certain Appius Claudius Russus, a forefather of the Julio-Claudian dynasty, "having set up his statue at Forum Appii with a crown upon his head, tried to take possession of Italy through his dependents." Russus certainly did not deserve a crown, but he did help spawn a long line of Claudians who made up Rome's first five emperors, from Augustus to Nero.

And I knew that Saint Luke the Evangelist, who presumably wrote the Acts of the Apostles in the Bible, said that he and Saint Paul, under guard by soldiers during that ill-fated journey to Rome, stopped here. "And the brethren there [Rome], when they heard of us, came as far as the Forum of Ap'pius and Three Taverns to meet us." Like crossing paths with Trajan, I would again come across Paul later in my journey through Northern Greece, known in ancient times as Macedonia.

Horace made time in his satire about his diplomatic journey along the Via Appia to talk about the two days he and his companions spent in Forum Appii. This was among the most entertaining parts of the work. The poet spoke of the drunken bargemen, their slaves, and "stingy innkeepers." He needed the delay because of "lousy water" that led his stomach to declare "war on me, and I wait impatiently while the others dined."

The bargemen carried passengers and plied their commercial wares along the canal running parallel to the Via Appia. They traveled back and forth between the sea and points inland, their craft being pulled by mules walking along the edges of the miles-long canal through the mosquito-infested Pontine Marshes. Horace does not describe Forum Appii but focuses instead on the inhabitants and the boatmen.

At this point in Roman history, nearly three hundred years after the Via Appia was first built, the road was in poor shape along this stretch. Horace and his companion decide to forego walking along the deteriorating surface and instead take a barge to Terracina, then spelled in the Latin "Tarracina." It also was known as Anxur, a name for the god Jupiter and his temple that Horace said is "perched on its cliffs that gleam brightly far and wide." They finally go to sleep on the tethered barge at night, despite the best efforts of the marsh frogs and "damned mosquitoes" to prevent sleep. And when they wake up, they discover the bargeman is passed out in a drunken stupor.

The Greek geographer Strabo wrote that "people navigate the canal preferably by night so that if they embark in the evening they can disembark early in the morning and go the rest of their journey by the [Appian] Way." This obviously was Horace's and his companion's plan: board in the evening and be at Anxur (Terracina) in the morning. But "when day dawns, we discover our vessel's not yet under way, till a hot-headed traveler leaps out thumping mule and man head and sides with a branch of willow." Horace seems to be subtly implying that he was that angry traveler.

By midmorning, the barge has landed and Horace and friends "wash our faces and hands in Feronia's stream," located in a sacred grove. Feronia is thought to be a Sabine goddess who was the consort to Anxurus, a youthful Jupiter. They shared a sanctuary in a grove near Terracina, with ponds of fresh water that attracted Horace. The Sabines were a pre-Roman Italic tribe. The conquering Romans adopted some of their religious practices and beliefs. There are those who equate Italic Feronia with Roman Diana and Greek Artemis.

The party of diplomats have breakfast and walk—Homer used the term "crawl"—the next three miles to Anxur. There they are met by Maecenas, Octavian's friend who served as his close adviser when he later became Emperor Augustus. They also meet up with Cocceius, a Roman diplomat who, in 40 B.C., had negotiated the Treaty of Brundisium that had divided the world among Octavian, Antony, and Lepidus.

The journey about which Horace is writing took place a few years after that original pact. Lepidus is by then out of the picture. This small group of diplomats, described by Horace as men who are "used to settling feuds between friends," would negotiate new terms for Antony and Octavian's relationship. That would become known as the Treaty of Tarentum. All these men were part of that delegation.

Horace tells us that Fonteius Capito, "a man so perfectly finished that Antony owns no greater friend than he" was with Cocceius. Interestingly, the friendship was so close that Antony, following the negotiations in Brundisium/Tarentum, dispatched Capito to Egypt to escort Queen Cleopatra to Antioch in Syria, where Antony had his headquarters as ruler of Rome's East.

My explorations of Borgo Faiti complete, I go to its bar and order my usual double espresso and sit outside in the early evening among tables of elderly men playing cards and folks having espressos, beers, and perhaps a small Italian cigar. A man sitting at the table next to me is smoking one, a Toscanello. He sees me admiring the small, flavorful delight and offers me one. I take it. He lights it for me. Conversation is impossible. He, no English. I, basic Italian, very basic. I nod in gratitude. The conversations around us are low, and their sound pleasantly fills the air around the front of the bar. It is September in Southern Italy, and the weather is clear and comfortable. I don't want to leave. Being immersed in a group of lovely people near the end of a perfect day makes me remember what Horace said as he rested among the frogs and mosquitoes of Forum Appii: "Night's already beginning to shroud the earth in shadow and sprinkle the heavens with stars." Eventually, as darkness slides down the foothills to the east and across the land to the sea, I decide I must leave.

I will spend the next few days in Terracina and visit Horace's destination—surely a destination of Caesar's and maybe Cicero's, on occasion—the Volscian Anxur, the Temple of Jupiter, sitting high above the coastal city with its vibrant Old Town neighborhood and its medieval buildings strung along the Via Appia, now a narrow but main artery with a grand name and covered in cobblestones.

5

TERRACINA AND ANXUR TO ITRI

There is no difference between Feronia and
Diana, just as there is no difference between
[Apollo] *Soranus and Iuppiter Anxur.*
—Archaeologist Massimiliano Di Fazio

I t is late. I spent too much time enjoying the early evening at that lovely bar in Borgo Faiti wondering if I indeed was sitting near where Horace's friends, more than two thousand years before, enjoyed their dinner while he battled his stomach tainted by bad water. I needed to get to Terracina, forty miles away, and find my lodgings for the night. Unlike Horace, I would travel on the Via Appia. The canal in front of the bar no longer offered mule-pulled barges for an overnight journey. I left in bright spirits, thanked the man at the next table for the Toscanello, set the B&B address in my navigator, and, fortified by a couple of double espressos, shot off down the famous road to that coastal city with the ancient temple to a "youthful" Jupiter.

Terracina is the first place where the Via Appia, at a point on the Gulf of Gaeta, touches the sea. An early name, according to Greek geographer Strabo, was Trachine, which he assumed was a derivative from the Greek word for "rugged." Horace and his contemporaries knew it, as we said earlier, by the Latin name Tarracina, but Horace referred to it only as Anxur. That is a place on Monte Sant'Angelo, high above the town, known as Jupiter Anxur.

It was the temple for Feronia's companion, the youthful Jupiter. It is not the sanctuary where he and Feronia frolicked in the mists of time. Its ponds and spring still exist—its significance is unknown by most everyone and tourists miss it completely—just off the Via Appia about three miles from the town, just as Horace said.

I drove past it a handful of times, not knowing it was there until after my journey. I am told there are no signs, just a grouping of four pools, with a freshwater spring that feeds them. This spring is likely "Feronia's stream," where he and his companions freshened up and ate breakfast.

A pre-Roman tribe known as the Volsci founded the village. Rome, growing greedy in its need to slowly bring the entire Italian Peninsula under its standard, took it over, beginning about 400 B.C. Over the centuries and well into the empire, Tarracina evolved into a resort where three emperors had villas. It included a large forum, a theater, baths, and a temple to Rome and Augustus. The temple high on the mountain, several hundred feet above the town, still exists in ruins restored and protected. The Roman ruins in the old town below also have been preserved and protected.

In ancient times, there were only three villages along where the ancient route met the sea before it crossed Southern Italy and reached those ports at the end, Taras (modern Taranto) and Brundisium (Brindisi). Beyond Terracina, on Italy's western coast, it passed through Formia, Minturnae (modern-day Minturno), and Sinuessa—places I would visit later.

After a brief search, I found the way to my rooms, named in Spanish "La Casita," or the Little House. I parked along the Corso Anita Garibaldi and hauled luggage into a dimly lit, tiny, pedestrian-only square, passing the entrance to a church, the Chiesa di San Giovanni, and, a few dozen feet later, found myself at the foot of two steep stone stairways. The irregularity of the steps looked as if they had been built in the Middle Ages. The door to the rooms had a keypad, and I had the code. It was late, close to midnight. The quarters were tight but comfortable. A steep wooden stair led to a loft and a bed. I opted to stay on the main floor with a comfortable-looking, wide couch equipped with adequate bedding. In the morning, I would contact my host, Roberto D'Ottavi, to check in. He would become a great friend and an informal but astute and highly educated tour guide.

We met for coffee at a tiny bakery next to the small square and sitting along the edge of the Corso Anita Garibaldi, named for the wife of one of Italy's 1861 unifiers, Giuseppe Garibaldi. In Roberto's basic English and my basic Italian, we talked about my journey along the Via Appia. He pointed to the slim roadway, the street alongside our outdoor table. "That is the Via Appia," he said. The one-way cobblestone street, seemingly too narrow to be named a "corso," covers the original route laid out by Claudius Appius in the third century B.C. It has become the main street through the middle of Terracina's old town.

Nice, I thought, to be spending nearly a week alongside the

very road I was writing about, where Caesar and other generals had led armies and Horace and his delegation likely traversed, after washing in Feronia's stream, to spend a night or two.

Roberto offered to show me around, and for each of the next five days, he spent a few hours with me as we wandered around his part of Terracina, the old part, not the modern postwar city spread out around this sea's edge. That first morning, we walked up the Corso Anita Garibaldi / Via Appia past the *capitolium* that had once been a small Roman temple dating to 50 B.C. and was dedicated to the Capitoline Triad: Jupiter, Juno, and Minerva. Now a small archaeological site, covered in scaffolding and surrounded by fences, it is undergoing restoration, *lavori in corso* (works in progress), and hard-hatted workers were on the site daily.

Directly across from it was a two-story medieval building with the remains of two Roman columns embedded in the outside walls. I wondered if it was built all those centuries ago on top of another Roman ruin? On its corner is a small museum with ancient mosaics. A few feet along, two small shops are carved out of a temple wall: a grocery and a souvenir shop, all part of structures created two millennia ago—repurposed and still in use.

We passed beneath a restored arch with a medieval building sitting high on top. This, in Roman times, was the entrance to the Emilian Forum, named after the magistrate who ordered it built, Aulus Aemilius. It was started in the late first century B.C. with work spilling over into the first century A.D. In many places, the forum's stone flooring is original. Now, portions of it are covered by seating for a restaurant, a bar at one end, and a gelato shop.

But the jewel in all this for me was the short section of original and preserved Via Appia. It runs the full length of the square, north to south. No motorized vehicles are allowed in the square, so this section is only walked on and, as I later learned, this stretch of ancient road is becoming a popular setting for wedding pictures.

At the far edge, it either disappears under buildings built over it in the Middle Ages or, when it resurfaces here and there, it again becomes part of a few paved streets. One end is flanked by the cathedral of Terracina, known as the Co-Cathedral of Saint Caesarius. It was formerly named for Saint Peter at its founding in the fifth and sixth centuries, when it was built atop the ruins of the Temple to Rome and Augustus. Its name was changed in the eleventh century for Terracina's patron saint, Saint Caesarius.

Then, Roberto took me by the arm and led me up some stone steps just above the original section of the Via Appia. At the top, I looked down to rows and rows of stone seats arrayed in a semicircle. This was a crescent-shaped Roman theater, he said, now surrounded on three sides by medieval structures that have been restored and modernized. Patrons sitting on those hard surfaces would have a view, above the performance platform, of the forum, its temple, and the sea beyond.

Roberto was laughing. "When do you think this was discovered," he asked. I had no idea. Was it sometime during the last two centuries when that kind of exploration and study became scientific?

Roberto continued. "As a child, I often played in a small square, which was located exactly where the theater cavea [the tiered half-circle seating space] is today. It was the early '50s; I think 1952 to '53. In the same years, the Italian scholar Aurigemma made the hypothesis of the existence of a theater in that place, having noticed the semicircular shape of the houses above and for the discovery of ancient walls, I suppose, in some cellars.

"The first excavations and systematic surveys began in 1968, and then from there began the clearance of the area with subsequent demolitions."

He told me that many Roman remains we now see around the forum were exposed during heavy Allied bombing from 1943 to 1944. The Allies wanted to disrupt travel between Naples and Rome and pound into submission Terracina's port, vital to enemy traffic along Italy's west coast. Things I saw over the next few days during my solo excursions up and down the Corso Anita Garibaldi / Via Appia—from in front of my rooms to the forum and treading on those original stones along the forum's edge—had been revealed, or at least hinted at, by that bombing. Horrible at the time for the people killed or displaced and their homes damaged or destroyed, it turned into something beneficial for later generations. Roberto, during one of our rambles around the old town area, showed me the toppled walls of a house high up in the town. This had been his grandmother's house, he said. Destroyed by bombs. Never repaired. She moved elsewhere.

Later, after a nice lunch sitting on those forum stones swept with early fall sunshine, we walked to the farther edge where a partial arch, probably damaged in the World War II bombing, ended the uncovered part of the preserved roadway. We walked along the modern streets on the portions that hid it below.

Roberto stopped at a small parking area with a wire fence closing off the end. Beyond the fence were the lawn and garden of a private estate. We looked through and there, perhaps 150 feet long, was another stretch of the exposed Via Appia. At the far end was another fence, and the entire length of the road was bordered by a high stone wall. It was completely enclosed. Imagine. A significant piece of Roman history in your backyard! I was glad to see that it appeared to be well taken care of.

A multistory structure sits on the forum's seaward edge, imposing and very modern amid Middle Ages architecture and splotches of antiquity. When patrons sat in the Greek-style theater on the other side, they would have had a view of the sea. No more. It is the *comune,* or city hall. It offers, through its lobby, its own arresting view of the modern city below, including a long stretch of road known as Via Appia Nuova. Beyond, toward the sea, twentieth-century structures, likely built after World War II Allied bombing, were spread out. And farther west sits the small harbor and the Gulf of Gaeta.

This port has early origins. It was one of a handful that Emperor Trajan wanted built along Italy's coasts at the beginning of the second century A.D. A new road branching off the Via Appia at the north end of the town could be built below the slope holding the original village, now what I refer to as old town, and along the water's edge. But it reached a spot where a high stony brow of Monte Sant'Angelo was too close to the water. That new road could not be extended around the brow to reconnect with the original Via Appia. So, what did the Roman engineers decide? They cut off the foot of the rock to create a thirty-foot-wide space for a road. It worked. The new byway was looped like a belt draped along the edge of the seafront, from one junction off the Via Appia at the north end of town to another junction tying it back in just beyond the south end. Trajan's version, which I often walked along looking for a place to eat or simply explore in the modern city, is known as Via Appia Nuova. Today the sea is much farther away. A modern slew of buildings and roads now sit on what was once the edge of the Gulf of Gaeta.

Roberto drove me to the spot where the rocky brow had been carved away. It was an impressive feat. Many tons of stone had been cut back to a height of 124 feet. And the engineers had to add a final touch: They built a wonderful arch over the road at the point where they had removed all that stone. The arch still stands, pressed against the mountain that Roman ingenuity conquered.

In one of our drives, Roberto headed up the northwest side of Monte Sant'Angelo, passing along a stone wall built more than two thousand years ago. I learned later that this was a Roman construction technique known as *opus incertum,* meaning it was designed both as a defensive wall and as a physical link connecting the town below with the Roman sanctuary on top. The Latin adjective refers to the construction design of the wall's facing of irregular polygonal blocks. This was a building technique—used between the third and first centuries B.C.— that I would see during this journey in walls still standing among the many ruins along the Via Appia.

Every few feet, as we drove along that wall, Roberto would point to a nub of stone sticking out of various sections. "A tomb," he would say. Then, a few feet farther along, "A tomb." We were heading toward the Temple of Jupiter, following the original Via Appia route, on roads with modern names. My friend said the temple area was closed, but he wanted to show me the route of the old, pre-Trajan course up to and across the top of the mountain.

At one spot, the pavement ended. We stopped. Before us was a small dirt road that was closed off a short distance away. Roberto said the rutted road, muddy after fall rains, was where the Via Appia Antica would have continued to the nearby town of Fundi, today's Fondi. Fundi was the next major stop for Horace and his diplomat friends. He deals with Anxur and Fundi in a few quick sentences, never saying how long they were here or whether they made it to the temple. He mentions Fundi only to make fun of the pompous airs of a man there who hosted them for dinner, Aufi'dius Luscus, the town's chief magistrate. Horace dismisses his political stature, saying he was only a "clerk" wearing a "bordered robe, a broad-striped tunic, burning charcoal." So much for kind words about a man hosting them for dinner and beds.

I would drive through Fondi, located a short distance inland from Terracina, in a day or so, before following the Via Appia as it slides down the Sant'Andrea della Valle along what was once a harsh and wild passage through the Aurunci Mountains to a stretch of the road along the Tyrrhenian Sea. But first, I wanted to wait for Temple of Jupiter Anxur to reopen, to see it on my own at a solitary pace, and to take in the magnificent views of the hills dropping down to the shocking blue water that seems to reach forever—views fit for the god of sky and thunder.

There was no thunder when I followed the drive up the mountain that Roberto and I had taken earlier, but rain, lightly falling as I left old town, had reached a boiling point when I got to the sanctuary atop the still-green mountain. I was dressed for it in a hooded waterproof coat and passed on the umbrella the kind ticket-office staff offered to loan. The area is well-kept with numerous paved pathways connecting each level.

Research had told me that this sanctuary was more than just a place to worship Jupiter. Its upper terrace had a military function. I saw where Romans had installed a military camp, including stone towers and more than a dozen vaulted cisterns.

The middle terrace was the religious center of the sanctuary. This is where weary pilgrims coming to honor the god would rest. The main temple, now long gone, and the rock of the oracle were there. All that remains are some fragments of statues, columns, Corinthian capitals, cornices, evidence of additional cisterns that are still used today, and a smattering of tiles. The only remains of the columned temple are some foundation blocks and a few traces of walls that had been built in the *opus incertum* style Roberto and I saw during our earlier drive up the mountain. That same construction style is found in pieces of additional walls found nearby.

On the lower level, reached by nicely constructed steps built in a way the Romans might have done, is what would be the "basement" of the temple above. This area faces south and looks over the city of Terracina, its port, and the Gulf of Gaeta far below. This view of the city and its layout, with old town clearly defined, put everything together for me.

Behind me were a series of still-present arches forming the wide basement of a temple that exists only in drawings and models. Before me—now that the rain had stopped and the clouds had scampered out of sight—was a spectacular mid-afternoon view offering a layout where I could imagine the ancient village around old town, the route of the Via Appia Antica through it all, and then Trajan's detour, today's Via Appia Nuova. I had struggled to make sense of it all as I had seen only close-up bits and pieces of the bigger picture. Here was the bigger picture, now nicely coming into focus.

Just before leaving Terracina, I had a goodbye caffè with Roberto. I had come to like being in this delightful seaside village full of remarkable history. But I had to quickly move on to Fondi, Horace's Fundi. Only about ten miles inland from Terracina, it would have been a day's walk for Horace and his companions. They stopped at the home of the village magistrate whom Horace had found pretentious. Instead of staying at an inn, Aufi'dius Luscus apparently offered them his home and fixed a meal for them, "burning charcoal" while dressed in fancy attire.

The Via Appia route I followed along the edges of the Aurunci Mountains into the city center appears to be on the original road, but the *Barrington Atlas* seems to indicate that cartographers are guessing at the precise route from a point southeast of Terracina to the edge of the town. Either way, SS7 must be close to, if not right on top of, the original road. There is a long, straight stretch approaching the town and, reaching the north edge of the center, the Via Appia/SS7 takes a sharp right turn and travels straight through it and nearly fourteen miles beyond to the coastal town of Formia, known in Roman times as Formiae.

My intention was to briefly explore Fondi's center and have lunch before moving out of the town in search of what friends had told me were walkable, preserved segments of the actual Roman road. The center is large, with attractive pedestrian-only streets and shops formed out of a collection of medieval buildings. It also houses a fourteenth-century castle, along with a cathedral that had been built over a Roman temple to Jupiter.

Its origin, according to legend, was at the hands of the strongman Hercules, a son of Jupiter. But reality and protohistoric evidence tell us it was originally settled by Latin peoples, probably around 1000 B.C. Subsequently, the Volsci, the folks who had founded nearby Terracina, arrived and occupied it, eventually giving way to the Romans. Rome gave the people citizenship in 188 B.C., more than a century after building the Via Appia through this area. Julius Caesar, in the first century B.C., would have regularly traveled through here, first as the young man on the rise in Roman society who was named curator of the road itself and later as the general who was establishing himself as dictator for life. His sometimes enemy / sometimes friend Cicero would have traveled it regularly between Rome and Formiae on the coast, where the orator had one of his nine villas. And later, in Christian times, it also doubled as a route known as the Via Francigena for pilgrims heading to Constantinople and Jerusalem.

The Roman military originally turned what is today Fondi's town center into a camp, a castrum, surrounded by walls forming a square. Its *decumanus,* or main town road, was, of course, the Via Appia. And today, the central axis of the square, the *decumanus maximus,* is named Corso Appio Claudio, after the builder of the *Regina Viarum.* This camp eventually grew into a place of temples and a forum. Eventually, from the fifth to the seventeenth centuries, popes laid claim to it, jousting at different times with the Kingdom of Naples over control. Fondi was on the border between papal lands and the empire ruled from Naples.

Interestingly, it was the site, in 1378, of the meeting where an antipope was elected, leading to the Great Schism that moved the papacy to France and lasted until 1417. And in more recent memory, World War II did not pass it by. The

Allies, thinking there were regiments of Germans in the city, bombed the center, damaging many of the historic structures. The only Germans there were recovering from wounds. The main army had moved north.

Between Fondi and the medieval-era town known as Itri and a bit beyond, roughly nine miles, original Via Appia segments still exist. They lie in a small valley through the Aurunci Mountains just off and parallel to SS7. Friends had told me that these sections, among the best preserved along the entire road's length from the end of Rome's *parco* to Brindisi, are perfect for short walks or bicycle journeys. The route is clear and well maintained, and signage is good at a couple of entry points.

Despite being in great shape for being 2,330 years old, the original surface stones we visualize when we think about Roman roadbuilding are missing in about seven of those nine miles. Many of the curbs are in place, and the original width has been kept up. I suspect a lot of those stones were gathered up beginning in the Middle Ages and used to build palaces for the well-to-do. This section of road had been rebuilt at least three times over the ensuing centuries. Roman emperor Caracalla ordered it done in 216; the viceroy of Naples, Pedro Afán de Ribera, did it in 1568; and Ferdinand IV, king of Naples at age eighteen, followed with improvements in 1768. The story is that he refurbished the road for the arrival of his bride, Maria Carolina of Austria. She had landed by ship at Terracina and, with her party in tow, traveled along the much-improved road. Until creation of the modern SS7, apparently the Via Appia through this valley was used until early in the twentieth century for regular travel, north and south, to the coast.

After lunch, I made the quick drive to Itri, about eight miles away. I would have time to explore only a small portion of the preserved Via Appia, and I knew that the two entrances just south of the village would be easily accessible. It was a good choice. I drove to the south end. A farm road that connects to the beginning of that preserved section plowed through a beautiful, youthful olive grove. Guard dogs greeted me, not with dire warnings in their barks but with hints of friendliness. Just off the road, a short distance from the beginning of the preserved section, a man and a woman were laying out fabric under olive trees, preparing the process of collecting a bountiful crop by shaking heavily laden branches. Itri, I discovered while talking to folks in a lovely restaurant called Osteria Murat there, is well-known for its olive oil. Groves packed with trees, their leaves shimmering silvery green, are everywhere along the hillsides between Fondi and Formia with Itri in between.

The fence declaring the end of the grower's property and the beginning of the protected section of roadway was just ahead. A large sign announced that this was indeed the restored Via Appia. The beginning was in an open area festooned with picnic tables, and the road began just across a low stone bridge over a small stream running through the narrow valley. It was obvious that driving along this section was forbidden; a gate closing it off to cars and just wide enough for a hiker or a bicyclist was ahead. I parked and started walking. It was straight and level through this valley bottom, and the comfortably warm day encouraged me to keep going.

I have no idea how far I trudged, but a stone ruin loomed up ahead. All I knew was that it was the Fort of Saint Andrew. Later, I learned while talking to a friend in Minturno when I was staying there over the following few days that it was built in the early eighteen hundreds by Murat, who was king of Naples. Murat, fearing that the French army would be coming through this valley to besiege him in Naples, chose the site because it once held a fourth-century B.C. Roman temple to Apollo. In the sixth century A.D., the church built a chapel on the temple's ruins. The temple and the chapel that replaced it were sturdy with stone walls built in the polygonal *opus incertum* style I had found at Anxur, above Terracina. The French, had they made it past Murat's fort, would not have been the only conquering army traveling down this narrow, mountainous valley. An article in Atlas Obscura says it most succinctly: "Starting in the 1500s, the wars over the Kingdom of Naples and of the Two Sicilies drew a significant number of Italian and foreign armies into this valley: Neapolitan, Papal, French, Spanish, Austrian, and German armies all marched on the basalt stones of the Appia Antica."

Jogging back to my car in a gentle, soothing rain, I drove north, back toward Itri to another entrance to the preserved Via Appia just a few miles away. This spot had a small parking area and a fence, but the gate was unlocked. I walked onto the preserved road and stared south down several hundred feet of roadway set at the Roman width standard of twenty to thirty feet. There were no large stones covering the top like those placed in 312 B.C., but the dirt and gravelly surface was rock-hard. I started walking past a series of signs offering bits of history and, interestingly, paintings of the different kinds of flowers and plants along the byway's edges: leccio (*Quercas ilex*) that was growing horizontally and then dropping vertically out of the rocky hillside; filirrea (*Phillyrea augustifolia*) with berries; and some I hadn't heard of before, terebinto

(*Pistacia terebintus*) and cisto (Cistus). Restorers had certainly done a wondrous job of making explanations about this section of a very old road helpful to visitors.

I could have walked back to Murat's fort from this direction, but the afternoon was wearing on, so I sat down on a mossy rock on the road's edge, looking across it toward the gully where a stream flowed far below. On the other side was the SS7, the road I would turn south on en route to the coastal town of Minturno and my next set of lodgings.

The road was not busy. There are nice breaks in traffic, and when this happens, the silence is overwhelmingly emotional. Only a breeze, a bird's chirp, the stream curling around stones far below. Again, I have those flights of amazement that I have experienced all over Italy when clobbered over the head with history. I am sitting on the edge of a road nearly twenty-three hundred years old—the pathway to war, commercial travel, pilgrimages of the faithful, its surface ruined and restored, over and over. Spartacus, leading his army from the north to the toe of Italy's boot in his ill-fated attempt to escape to Sicily, likely rode through here; Caesar was here many times; a century or so later, Saint Paul the Apostle walked by my spot, under guard, on his way to certain death in Emperor Nero's Rome. And I could almost see Horace and his companions tramping by on their way to Brundisium and Tarentum to hopefully patch things up between Octavian and Mark Antony. Their Treaty of Tarentum failed in the long run, but we are left with a description of a sweet journey along a road that according to one information sign "is a perfect mix between landscape and history, nature, and archaeology."

6

CICERO

There looms ahead a tremendous contest between them
[Caesar and Pompey]. Each counts me as his man,
unless by any chance one of them is pretending. . . .
What is more, I received letters from both of
them . . . conveying the impression that neither has
a friend in the world he values more than myself.
But what am I to do. . . . I am clear that defeat
with one is better than victory with the other.
                    —Roman lawyer, writer, and statesman Cicero

C oming down from the Aurunci Mountains and following a relaxing hour in Itri sitting on a bench alongside the paved-over Via Appia, drinking a *portare via*
(takeaway) double espresso and admiring a view of the town's
medieval castle, I came out of the Gola di Sant'Andrea and
dropped down onto the coastal range and into the town of
Formia. My destination was Minturno, just a few miles beyond, where I had reserved a room for three days. This coastal
area—ranging from Formia, Minturno, and a site known in
ancient times as Sinuessa, now lodged in the modern village
of Mondragone—all tie into my efforts to follow the journey

of Horace and his party on their way to resolve differences between Octavian and Mark Antony.

The travelers stayed in Formia, then known as Formiae. Horace called it "Mamurra's town." Ancient Romans reading the satire would know who Mamurra was. He is described as a Roman knight who was "a notorious favorite of Julius Caesar . . . [and] was Caesar's chief engineer in Gaul." Mamurra became incredibly wealthy working for the general and future dictator of Rome. He died in 44 B.C., perhaps eight years before Horace's trip and just one year before Caesar's murder.

Apparently, a gentleman, Aulus Terentius Varro Murena— the brother-in-law of Horace's companion Maecenas—"offered shelter" in Formiae. Years later, in the earliest days of the empire, Murena was nominated as consul with Augustus for 23 B.C. But Murena died before he could take office. There was a long line of luxurious Roman villas from Formiae to the sea at Gaeta, and Murena's likely was one of those. A member of Horace's group, Mark Antony's close friend Fonteius Capito, handled "the cooking." Then, with no more detail about that one-night visit, Horace, in his satire, jumps to the next morning:

> The next day's sunrise brings great joy: since Plotius, Varius, and Virgil, meet us at Sinuessa: no more shining spirits did earth ever bear, and no one could be more dearly attached to them than I. O what embraces there were there, and what delight!

These three, who must have landed by boat, would join the party for the push inland to Capua, thence to Beneventum and on to Brundisium and Tarentum. Plotius Tucca and Lucius Varius Rufus were close friends of the poet Virgil, who, in the years following Horace's journey, was commissioned by Emperor Augustus to write Rome's foundation myth, the *Aeneid*. Virgil died in 19 B.C. before he finished and, on his deathbed, asked his friends to burn the manuscript. He thought it was a poor effort. They didn't, and upon orders from the emperor, they edited and published it.

Horace does not mention any of the places the group passed through from Formiae to Sinuessa. He leaves out Minturnae, the precursor to my destination Marina di Minturno just a few miles south. In his time, Minturnae was large and columned with the usual temples, squares, baths, and forums. This archaeological site remains. And the Via Appia Antica runs straight through it, perfectly preserved with its stones and curbs intact. The town moved up the surrounding hillside sometime during the ninth or tenth century, likely using building stones from the ancient city and hastening its transformation into a ruin. I chose modern Marina di Minturno, north of the protected remains and along the water of the Tyrrhenian Sea, and not the town's namesake higher on the hill. I wanted to remain close to the Via Appia.

As I approached Formia, I kept an eye out for a tall stone structure on the side of the road that borders the Gulf of Gaeta. I saw it and pulled over on the very narrow edge of the SS7, barely out of the way of traffic. Here, the two-lane highway follows the precise route of the Via Appia. There is no parking at this site, and I suspected the gate to the fence surrounding it was closed. This is the Tomb of Cicero, the great Roman orator, lawyer, and former consul of Rome whose loyalties shifted like morning to night between powerful Romans, including Julius Caesar and the general's eventual enemy Pompey.

Cicero had a villa here—one of the nine his biographer, Anthony Everitt, said he owned around Italy. Various authorities disagree whether any of the ruins of Roman-era villas in the area were Cicero's, but I suspect it was near Murena's where Horace's party stayed the night.

Caesar and Pompey, at different times over the years, often visited Cicero at Formiae. Cicero was killed somewhere near this so-called tomb. But almost everyone who studies Roman history—and especially the history of the period that encompasses the dying embers of the republic—believes he is nowhere to be found inside the eighty-foot-tall tomb, its tower sitting on a square base. Many call it a monument; a few believe it marks the spot where he was murdered on the orders of Mark Antony. Whatever it is, it is photogenic and sits on beautiful grounds filled with Mediterranean greenery and a grove of olive trees. I had read that the gate is rarely open to visitors, perhaps one day a month for a few hours. My timing was off. I couldn't get in and climbing the iron fence in full view of this busy roadway did not seem like the right thing to do.

Cicero, born in 106 B.C., was about six years older than Caesar. His family, while wealthy, was not part of the ruling class. Caesar was from that upper class, the patricians, but he was not necessarily wealthy. Cicero, known in Roman society as novus homo (new man), was educated in Rome and Greece, so he spent much of his life traveling back and forth along the Via Appia. He had to work extra hard and train himself as an orator and lawyer so he could stand out in Roman society—and he had to marry well. He did. He married Terentia, wealthy in her own right while her husband was financially imprudent. She pushed Cicero to action against powerful enemies and ran his many households. For thirty years, she was his main benefactor. Cicero's biographer, Anthony Everitt, describes her as "a strong-minded woman [who] perhaps felt she had to take decisive action if something were to be saved from [Cicero's] financial wreckage."

They eventually divorced with Cicero blaming her, not himself, for their financial problems.

Cicero's rise was meteoric. He held a series of offices and in 63 B.C. was elected consul. He was the youngest Roman to reach the highest political office in the republic. That year, 63 B.C., marked one of his early rifts with Julius Caesar and set him on a path to earn Mark Antony's wrath. Caesar twice supported Lucius Sergius Catilina in 64 and 63 B.C. for a consulship. He lost both times. Cicero won in 63. Eventually, a group of Catilina's supporters fomented a rebellion in his support. As consul, Cicero demanded that the men, involved in what became known as the Catiline Conspiracy, be executed without trial. Caesar objected, advocating instead imprisonment. Caesar lost, and the senate ordered the men executed. One of the conspirators Cicero had executed was Mark Antony's stepfather. Much later, Cicero, in 43 B.C., wrote fourteen hostile speeches against Antony. A bad decision indeed.

Consuls served only for a year, and Caesar, at age forty, was elected in 59 B.C. Here's where tradition went by the wayside. Caesar formed an alliance with Crassus—the general who defeated Spartacus—and with another general, Pompey, who married Caesar's daughter, Julia, in 59. This became known as the First Triumvirate. It ruled for six years. Cicero, an ardent believer in the republic, objected. None of the three, in Cicero's view, would be the proper champion for the survival of the republic.

Crassus eventually died, and tensions increased between Caesar and Pompey—Julia had died at a young age, and family ties were diminished—and that would lead to a civil war in 49 B.C. This is when both men sought to curry Cicero's favor. His villa at Formiae drew the adversaries for visits—conveniently for Cicero, at different times. One source says Pompey and Cicero accidentally bumped into each other in Campania where Pompey was raising troops to fight Caesar. Together they went to Formiae.

Sometime after that meeting, Caesar stopped by the villa with a contingent of at least two thousand soldiers as a guard and escort in hopes of winning Cicero over. The philosopher had to billet and feed those two thousand and complained to his friend Atticus about the imposition. The historian Mary Beard describes Caesar's visit in fascinating detail, including his bath and massage and how he had a huge appetite at dinner. She opined: "Once is enough. The best that one can observe is that entertaining a victorious Pompey would almost certainly have been just as much bother."

But Cicero chose to side with Pompey. Caesar won that civil war, Pompey went off to exile in Egypt where he was murdered, and the now dictator-for-life met Cicero on the Via Appia outside the gates of Brundisium, offering forgiveness.

Cicero certainly had nothing to do with Caesar's murder a few years later, and he expressed revulsion at what had happened on the Ides of March. But he supported, after the fact, the assassins, saying, "Our tyrant deserved his death," because Caesar was ambitious to be "king of the Roman people and master of the whole world." This, Cicero said, made Caesar into "a madman."

Cicero was hopeful this would set Rome back on track toward being a republic and divert it away from empire. He was wrong. Mark Antony and Caesar's grandnephew and heir Octavian eventually developed ideas of their own. Cicero had done little to become friendly with Antony, calling him a tyrant in those various speeches and, while he liked Octavian, he called for him to be removed. Historian Tom Holland, in

Rubicon: The Last Years of the Roman Republic, described the widening fissure with Antony thusly:

"Why should it have been my fate," Cicero pondered, "that for the past two decades the Republic has never had an enemy who did not turn out to be my enemy as well?" . . . By denouncing Antony, he was effectively declaring war not on an open rebel . . . but on a man who was himself the head of state. But Cicero was unabashed . . . he believed himself confronted by a monster. . . . So it was that Cicero, the spokesman of legitimacy, prepared to work for the destruction of a consul.

This ended up with Cicero on a "wanted" list and certain death. Antony saw to it and sent soldiers after Cicero, who was resting at his villa in Formiae before going into exile in Greece. Knowing the soldiers were after him, he and his litter bearers headed through the woods off the Via Appia toward Gaeta and the sea. Somewhere along that stunning coastline, they caught up to him. Just a year after Caesar's murder and a year before Antony and Octavian defeated Caesar's killers at Philippi in Macedonia, Cicero was beheaded. Antony ordered his head and right hand displayed as trophies on the rostrum in the Roman Forum, the very spot where Caesar's remains had been cremated and the scene of many of the brilliant orations that Cicero had delivered to the Roman people. A poor ending for one of Rome's greatest philosophers.

Standing along the wall, on the outside of his so-called tomb, I wondered when it was built. A quick check on the world of information available through my phone says it dates to the second half of the first century, roughly a century after his death. That puts it in the time frame of the apostle Paul's journey to Rome, arriving in A.D. 60. Perhaps this monument to Cicero was brand-new when Paul and Luke, strode by, under Roman guard.

It was time to move on. My car's navigator took me to my rooms in Marina di Minturno, a mostly postwar extension spread out along the water and down the hill from the medieval town. I preferred the more modern Marina area because the Via Appia/SS7 runs through its middle. It would be only a few dozen feet away. Nearby, just before the historic Garigliano River that serves as the boundary between the regions of Lazio and Campania, sit the ruins of Minturnae. This was the ancient Roman town that Horace and his party, after breakfast in Formiae, quickly passed through, eager to meet Virgil and his two friends a few miles farther south in Sinuessa.

I spent three days in Marina di Minturno, likely more time in one spot than Horace spent in all three villages his group traveled through. How they made the trip at this point is not revealed. The next time Horace would mention any kind of mode to travel was the use of pack mules, which "shed their loads early" in Capua, almost due east from Sinuessa. One translation of the satire has the mules "laying aside their saddle bags at an early hour."

We can only speculate that most of the journey, except for the barge ride down the canal from Forum Appii to Terracina, was a combination of by foot and by mules, roughly covering between nine and fifteen miles a day. In addition, the wealthier members of the party, Maecenas and Capito, whom Horace met in Terracina, could have had slaves handling baggage. After Capua, all the principals in the diplomatic delegation probably continued, seated on the backs of mules. Horace certainly spares his reader significant detail.

My time in Minturno was mostly spent at the nearby ruins of the ancient town and wandering along the Garigliano River, which has a transfixing history. Long before the Romans were around, the indigenous people worshiped a river goddess known as Marica. This was her river when it was called the Liris. She was a goddess of enchantment, spell craft, and transformation. One source tells us that she also was a goddess of wildwood and salt marshes, along with the wildlife that frequents such places. That rang a familiar bell: I thought of my old friend Diana. A little more research revealed that Marica was also worshiped by Romans after they arrived, and some Roman authors claimed that she was a form of Diana or Venus, a goddess whom Julius Caesar claimed as an ancestor.

The name Marica is a descriptive title and not a proper name like Diana or Apollo. In a pre-Roman language, it roughly translates to "goddess of the salt marshes." She had a temple, mythologists believe, and in the 1920s searchers discovered foundations in what was once a marsh that could be the site of her temple. They also uncovered votive figurines that could be associated with her. Driving along that riverbank there is no obvious evidence that her temple was ever there. No signs led the way, just modern campgrounds and parking areas for beach access.

Marica's association with this sweet-flowing, twenty-five-mile-long river, rising in the mountains to the east, is not its only claim to history. In addition to setting the boundary between two regions of Italy, it also served, in the Middle Ages when it was called the Verde River, as the southern boundary of the Papal States.

This is important to note because fewer than five centuries after the end of the Roman Empire a new ruling dichotomy of competing powers had developed and was growing. The pope controlled various areas of Southern Italy, as did the Lombards and Byzantines. The river, the rich area, and towns near it also became an attraction for a new power. The Muslims were in the process, between 827 and 902, of taking over Sicily from the Byzantines. They became established in Palermo, which, according to *A History of Muslim Sicily,* "increased Muslim naval activity along the coast of Italy." Eventually, they were "hired by the Neapolitans to assist them to resist the attacks of . . . the Lombard prince of Benevento." Their base was at the foot of Mount Vesuvius.

This means the "Muslims were officially invited to intervene in the political turmoil of southern Italy." They became mercenaries serving the interests of the major power players in the region. After helping the Neapolitans, they eventually started turning on their hosts. Byzantine Naples and Lombard Salerno joined forces and drove them out. And sometime in the early 880s, at the invitation of the powers that be in Gaeta, just west of Formia, they established a base at the mouth of the Garigliano River where today sit campgrounds and delightful beaches. Gaetani wanted their help because they were nervous about outside influences, being so close to the southern edge of the Papal States and with Capua, ruled by Lombards, not too far away. They invited the Muslims to settle along the river.

For seventy-five years, the various rulers in the larger areas around Naples and Minturno and farther east had tolerated Muslim mercenaries to help them keep interlopers at bay. Then, the band based at the Garigliano began to show aggression toward their benefactors. They raided deep within papal territory and began harassing the folks who had once welcomed them. In 903, an alliance was created to deal with the growing threat. It started with Capua, Naples, and Amalfi joining to attack the Garigliano base. The Muslims won that battle and the informal triumvirate regrouped, this time persuading Gaeta to join forces.

Gaeta's leaders, still nervous about a potential threat from Capua and not sure they wanted to bid the Muslims farewell, were offered a choice plum by a new pope, John X. He promised the Gaetani total sovereignty over two hundred square miles of coastal land that was part of the Papal States, from Terracina to the mouth of the Garigliano. The rulers of Gaeta accepted and promised they would not oppose the combined force of soldiers from the papal army, Capua, Benevento, and Salerno, along with some Byzantines and other peoples. This conglomeration of forces, in the spring of 915, surrounded the camp while a Byzantine fleet guarded the mouth of the river, cutting off Muslim escape by sea. It took three months, but the camp was wiped out. The joining of forces by these disparate and often combatant armies led to a more cooperative relationship. At least for a while.

I parked a short distance from the river's mouth and contemplated all this history. I wish, in retrospect, I could have found the spot of Marica's temple and wonder if those foundation stones were still there. I imagined that the Muslim encampment did not have stone structures or anything permanent. My friend, Dr. Leonard Chiarelli—a foremost authority and author of *A History of Muslim Sicily*—says they likely lived in tents, perhaps on the beach area I was parked at nearby. "There would be no trace," he said, evidence of their presence blowing in the wind like the desert sands of their faraway home.

What *are* here, with stones too heavy to be blown away like the Muslim tents, on the north side of the river and a few hundred feet from the modern Via Appia/SS7, are the ruins of Minturnae. This site, fewer than two miles from the river's mouth and with what was once Marica's sacred glen likely within shouting distance, is well marked and maintained.

During my time there, virtually alone as I was the only visitor in the four hours I spent wandering, I was greeted by a friendly threesome of ticket takers. One spoke English, and she directed me to the entrance of the site. The seating area of the Roman theater looked newer than I would have expected. "Bombs," she said, referring to World War II. The Garigliano, after all, was the so-called Gustav Line, one of Germany's lines of defense, and a serious target of Allied bombing. "It is remade, like it was," she said pointing to the rows of seats.

In researching the site, I learned that the restored theater was inaugurated in 1960, with the Euripides play *The Trojan Women*. That would have been a great thing to see, in that setting, among the ruins of an ancient town with the original Via Appia cutting through it. Patrons would be looking over that restored roadway, wide and with its curbs intact, and on to the Tyrrhenian Sea beyond. Horace and his fellow travelers would have quickly passed by this spot as they went through Minturnae en route to Sinuessa, just fifteen miles south. There, they would meet the poet Virgil and his two companions.

I gathered resources from various historians to fill me in on the history. Roberto Piperno of Rome is a thorough researcher as are the writers for *The Princeton Encyclopedia of*

Classical Sites. The ticket office had little information—just a small basic brochure in Italian—and I had to look elsewhere for the details about what I was seeing as I wandered among the tumbled stones of the theater, the forum, and the baths.

There was an earlier town here, perhaps settled in the seventh century B.C., before the Romans, and archaeologists have found no trace of it. We know about it because it was mentioned by the Roman historian Livy, who wrote a monumental history of Rome. He said the Romans conquered the original inhabitants, the Ausonians, in 313 B.C. This was one year before the beginning of the Via Appia, and builders reached this area about two years later, in 311. By 296 it was a Roman village. A castrum, or fort, was built alongside the road, perhaps on top of the destroyed Ausonian village. The Carthaginian general Hannibal, during the Second Punic War, was terrorizing the area at different points during his nearly fifteen-year (219–203 B.C.) failed effort to conquer Rome, and Minturnae was reinforced with walls and towers before 207.

Eventually, it became one of the colonies where veterans of the armies of Julius Caesar—and later Augustus—were allowed to claim land as a reward for their service. Augustus, or perhaps his successor Tiberius, had an aqueduct built to bring water from Mount Aurunci nearly seven miles away to the east. Sections still stand today near the medieval town of Minturno on the hillside above Marina di Minturno and the ruins. The emperors also built the theater with more than four thousand seats. Temples were added, and, of course, statues of the emperor—archaeologists are not sure which one—were added.

Warring factions, in the late sixth century A.D., led to its destruction. The Lombards usually get the blame. Survivors relocated to a nearby hill, but the Muslims, different from the ones who had settled at the mouth of the Garigliano three centuries later, destroyed that spot.

I wondered about the bridge the Romans had to have built over the then-named Liris River to carry the Via Appia farther south. In the late 1960s, archaeologists conducted underwater surveys and found wooden pilings and concrete rubble of what Cicero called, in a letter to his friend Atticus, Pons Tirenus. This bridge did not survive, and others likely were built over the centuries.

In the late eighteenth century, English antiquarian Sir Richard Colt Hoare wrote that there was no bridge across the river "but only a ferry at a large tower; a little higher up are the remains of a bridge, but it is not known when it was built, or when destroyed." I was drawn to Hoare because he and an artist companion, Carlo Labruzzi, were trying to do what I was doing—follow Horace's journey from Rome to Brindisi. Hoare didn't make it beyond Benevento; he took ill and, also burdened by bad weather, had to abandon his trip.

But he wrote about Minturnae without judgment. It was "rendered interesting to us, even though in ruins, by the local history and classical anecdotes connected with it." About the same decade as Hoare's journey, the German writer Johann Wolfgang von Goethe, traveling through Italy and Sicily, was not so kind. He called the site a "nameless and orderless mass of ruins." And still another traveler during that same time frame, English writer Henry Swinburne, loved the sight of the Garigliano River but was not impressed by the ruins:

> I descended into a spacious plain, open to the Sea, and clothed with rich crops of corn; the few uncultivated spots were over-grown with cistus in full flower and fragrance. The Garigliano flowing silently out of the mountains,

traverses the vale in a deep winding bed, and empties itself into the sea, a little below the ruins of Minturnae, which made an awful appearance along its banks.

Today, there are two bridges that carry traffic and pedestrians southward. The modern bridge was built in the 1960s; the much older Real Ferdinando Bridge was built in 1832 by the Naples-based Kingdom of the Two Sicilies. They are side by side, but the older structure, a suspension bridge with two towers on each bank of the Garigliano, is restricted except for pedestrians. I walked out of the parking lot of the Minturnae ruins and across the road to the gate for the bridge's historic site. It was surrounded by a high construction fence with a sign saying, in direct language: CLOSED! It was under major repair. And there was no indication when it would open. This bridge likely is near the spot where Cicero's Pons Tirenus, given the archaeological discoveries of the late 1960s, had been constructed by the Romans to carry the Via Appia over the river.

Like his brief, one-sentence mention of Formiae, Horace expends almost no words on Sinuessa, just a few miles south of Minturnae. He mentions that he met Virgil and his companions there and went a few miles eastward where they spent the night at a "small villa" by the Pons Campanus (Campanian Bridge) that offered "shelter, and the officers, as required, salt and fuel."

This bridge crossed the Savo River, today known as the Savone, a small stream that empties into the sea a few miles south of Sinuessa. Then, after crossing another branch of the Savo, they reached the Volturnus (Volturno) River valley and followed it to ancient Capua, today's Santa Maria Capua

Vetere. By telling us that the mules shed their loads early, they must have arrived before the day grew late, offering plenty of time for rest.

And he must have known that they were traveling through an area that an earlier writer, Pliny the Elder, had identified as Ager Falernus, part of the northern Campanian countryside famous for its wines. Pliny was among several Romans praising the grape; Horace and Virgil also wrote that it was among the finest they had tasted. Perhaps they had some at that inn by the Pons Campanus.

Sinuessa offers only a small plot of ruins within the village of Mondragone—and just a few miles south the Via Appia leaves the Tyrrhenian Sea for the last time. A short, rough section of the original road, still covered with its famous stones, is found in these ruins with the remains of what could have been a triumphal arch; fragments of buildings are scattered about.

The modern road that crosses the Garigliano River at Minturno and heads south has a slightly different designation, SS7qtr. The regular SS7, which I had been following since Rome, diverges from the ancient route at Minturno. Instead of heading south, the direction that Horace and his companions traveled, it turns southeast through hills and plains and flows onward to Santa Maria Capua Vetere.

Today, from Mondragone/Sinuessa almost directly eastward, there is a small collection of provincial roads weaving their way through the Volturnus (Volturno) River valley to Santa Maria Capua Vetere. It is interesting that none of these provincial roads bear any reference to the Via Appia. In fact, the *Barrington Atlas of the Greek and Roman World* shows a dotted line representing the route through this area. That means the mapmakers are guessing at its location. The segment seems to be in hiding along this short stretch of about twenty-four miles. The most direct road to Santa Maria Capua Vetere is SP333, which, like the ancient road, has several straight sections through the river valley.

The SS7qtr, south from the Garigliano Bridge and well past Mondragone, is known as the Via Domiziana. This is the modern name for the Via Domitiana, a Roman road built in A.D. 95, more than a century after Horace's journey, beginning at the adjacent ports of Puteoli (modern Pozzuoli) and Portus Julius (modern Baiae), and supplanting the much older Via Appia north to Minturnae, roughly thirty-eight miles. The Via Domitiana, now the SS7qtr, is purely a coastal road, allowing bygone travelers from Puteoli and beyond to head straight to Rome without the eastward loop to ancient Capua and back again.

Hannibal, the Carthaginian general, ranged freely about this countryside. After crossing the Alps and entering Italy, his army had defeated the Romans in two significant battles north of Rome: along the Trebbia River in late 218 B.C., then at Lake Trasimene in the spring of 217 B.C. By September, flush with those significant victories, the general moved his army south into Campania. He reportedly came up to the gates of Sinuessa, apparently keeping the town intact while ravaging the countryside along the Via Appia and the hills and valleys to the east.

In this area known as Ager Falernus, Hannibal met the Romans, who surrounded him but held off attacking. He, using a variety of tricks, eventually found a way to break out. This ended what has become known as the Battle of Ager Falernus, essentially viewed by historians as a small but significant episode.

The consul in charge of the Roman army, Quintus Fabius Maximus Verrucosus, chased the Carthaginians eastward toward the Adriatic but had little success in stopping them. He and his army would likely come to regret their hesitation to forcibly engage. Eleven months later, in August 216 B.C., Hannibal would confront a massive Roman army at the Battle of Cannae, and, through decisive strategy, win one of the greatest battles in history.

The countryside around Sinuessa recovered over time, of course, and by the time Horace and his group hooked up with Virgil nearly 180 years later, they could enjoy their journey and likely imbibe one of the peninsula's finest wines. What is known about the village, of which today only a few clusters of stone remain along with a rough remnant of the ancient Via Appia running through it, is that it began as a Roman colony around 296 B.C.

Cicero wrote about it, and historians say that Julius Caesar, in 49 B.C., stopped there for the night. The Greek geographer Strabo said that "near Sinuessa are hot baths, which are most efficacious for certain diseases." Pliny the Elder, much earlier, wrote that these baths cured barrenness in women and insanity in men. They were called Aquae Sinuessanae. Livy mentioned them as early as the Second Punic War with Hannibal. The site still exists, along with the ruins of Roman buildings. Thermal baths still operate in the area, but Strabo's translator is quick to point out, in a curious footnote, that he doesn't know whether the modern baths can be identified with those found in ancient times.

I needed to go to Santa Maria Capua Vetere and beyond to Benevento. There I would turn south on the Via Appia/SS7 to Horace's birthplace, Veniusa (modern Venosa) where the road bisects the village and now is lined with wonderful medieval structures in an old town worth visiting. In the eleventh century, the Abbey of the Most Holy Trinity in Venosa was patronized by Normans, and Robert Guiscard and others are interred in what became a dynastic tomb, the family's first place in Italy. This contributed to the medieval resettlement and expansion of the town that had been in decline after the Romans.

Horace did not head in that direction, missing Venusia. He and his party left the Via Appia at Beneventum and headed southeast on a series of rutted pathways to the coast and then to Brundisium. They knew that the new route, which nearly 150 years later would become the Via Traiana, was through countryside that was mostly level compared with the Via Appia's more tortuous route through hills and valleys. The detour did not save the party much time, since it was a bit longer, but it likely was far more comfortable.

7

THE CITY OF VENUS

Carpe diem quam minimum credula postero.
(Pluck the day, trusting as little as
possible in the next one.)

—Roman poet Horace

Horace and his party arrived early in Capua riding mules, while servants on foot who were more likely slaves led the pack animals loaded with baggage. He tells us in his satire that "Maecenas is off for sport, Virgil and I for sleep: Those ball-games are bad for sore eyes and stomachs. Then Cocceius' well-stocked villa welcomes us, that overlooks the inns of Caudium."

Maecenas, in his early thirties and eager to play ball, was a close friend and adviser to Octavian, the future emperor, hence his need to make the diplomatic journey on behalf of his friend. He was just five years older than Horace, then in his late twenties, who seems throughout the satire to be quite sedentary and sluggish and suffering from stomach issues and tired eyes. It appears that almost no time at all was spent in that town. In the next sentence following the one about Maecenas's need for sport, they are guests at a villa at Caudium (modern Montesarchio), about twenty-seven miles from ancient Capua (today known as Santa Maria Capua Vetere) and eighteen miles west of Beneventum.

Horace leaves us locked in a mystery here. Let's back up. In a few quick sentences, he has his group leaving the inn at Pons Campanus just inland from coastal Sinuessa, arriving early in Capua and then stopping for a ball game and apparently a nap for him and Virgil. Then they are in a villa overlooking Caudium. From Pons Campanus to Caudium is roughly forty miles on modern roads that generally follow the ancient route. That leaves a lot to the imagination about the time frame and their rate of travel, and it burrows into my imagination as I pass through these places.

Unlike Horace, I will spend a few days in Santa Maria Capua Vetere. It is, after all, where Spartacus trained as a gladiator and began the massive slave revolt in 73 B.C. that ended with six thousand of his ex-slave soldiers crucified along the 132-mile length of the Via Appia, from Rome to Capua, where it all started. That is about forty-five crucifixions per mile or, roughly, one every seventeen feet. Certainly doable when you have an army, as the victorious Roman general Crassus did, with time on their hands.

Santa Maria Capua Vetere strikes the weary traveler as ordinary. Driving in along the Via Appia Nuova/SS7 that cuts through the town's center, I saw a pleasant place with many shops and churches. Nothing stands out as medieval, except for a few of the churches. Its architecture mostly seems postwar. If you miss the turn where my rooms can be found, perhaps 150 yards off the SS7, and continue, you will find yourself in adjoining Caserta, which the Lombards founded in the eighth century A.D. According to the Roman historian Cato the Elder, the Etruscans, who were far afield from their natural homeland near Rome, founded neighboring Capua around 600 B.C.

I knew one fact about Caserta. Its eighteenth-century royal palace, Reggia di Caserta—by volume, the largest palace in the world—was the headquarters for the Allied Forces Mediterranean command during World War II. From airfields sprinkled around the countryside, Allied bombers took off, daily bombing targets far and wide as the Germans were driven higher and higher up the boot. Historian James Holland, in *Italy's Sorrow: A Year of War, 1944–1945*, reminds us that more Italians were "killed by Allied bombing, shellfire, and strafing than were being slaughtered by the Germans." And this was after Italy became an ally. War is certainly an act of extreme barbarism. Caserta was the palace where the Germans, on April 29, 1945, signed their surrender of troops in Italy. The final surrender of all German troops in Europe took place eight days later, May 7, in Reims, France.

In further reading, I learned that it was around Santa Maria Capua Vetere and Caserta that Giuseppe Garibaldi, in the effort to unify Italy, fought the Battle of the Volturno in 1860, defeating Neapolitan forces.

But long before these more modern battles and wars, numerous collisions between mighty powers were fought around this area of south-central Italy over the centuries. This included when the Romans defeated native peoples in 340 B.C., just three decades before the Via Appia was completed to this point. They made Capua and other villages into colonies ruled from Rome. Capuani were given limited Roman citizenship, meaning they became Romans in almost every sense of the word but could not vote or hold elective office, and the village prospered, becoming Italy's second largest after Rome.

This also was part of the countryside where the Carthaginian general Hannibal roamed at will after his first three major victories farther north and his army's escape from that weak Roman encirclement near Sinuessa. After Rome's crushing defeat at Cannae, Capua's leaders felt Hannibal would win the war. He brought his army to their precinct and made it his winter quarters. Roman historian Livy says that while here, Hannibal addressed the people of Capua and told them he would make their town the capital of Italy, and everyone, including the conquered Romans, would adhere to Capua's laws. The townsfolk liked hearing that and threw their support behind Hannibal, betraying the Romans. That did not sit well after Rome finally was able to drive him out of Italy in 203 B.C. Capua and many other villages that offered the Carthaginians support over the fifteen years Hannibal's army roamed the peninsula suffered mightily when Romans reasserted control.

The names of the modern towns can be confusing to the unwary traveler. My friend, historian Lou Mendola, told me that the town that holds the name Capua today took that name in A.D. 856 prior to the era of Norman rule in Sicily and Southern Italy. It is here where alliances get tricky. Ancient Capua had been destroyed by Saracens, mercenaries who had been employed by the Lombard ruler of Benevento, who in turn was an ally of the Berber amir of Bari, Khalfun. It was he who led the assault against Capua. Its surviving residents moved three miles northward to the Roman town of Casilinum and gave it the ancient name. The original Capua became known as Santa Maria Maggiore, named after one of the great churches there. Then, in 1861, under Italian unification, the name was changed again to reflect its ancient past, becoming

Santa Maria Capua Vetere, with "Capua Vetere" meaning Old Capua.

I begin, the morning of my second day, to explore the city. The evening before, my host, Antonio Ianniello, drove me around the neighborhood just off the Via Appia/SS7. He pointed out the city's various highlights: a museum, the circular Roman amphitheater where Spartacus fought as a gladiator, the remains of various baths, and a theater. In passing, he mentioned that the god Mithra was worshiped here. Foolishly, I didn't ask him about what I would assume to be temple ruins. I felt they would be somewhere near the amphitheater. All these places were in the same general area and within walking distance. The next morning, after caffè and a cream-filled croissant, I struck out on foot toward the Roman ruins.

The amphitheater was a marvelous sight. On the approach were comfortable-looking gardens and walkways being tended by a group of volunteer gardeners, pulling weeds, trimming bushes, spading the soil. I bought a ticket and wandered through the ancient entrance and could almost hear the roar of the crowd. I've been in a few of these kinds of places: the Colosseum in Rome; amphitheaters in Siracusa, Sicily; Roman Carthage in Tunisia; and Pompeii; and theaters in Heraclea Lyncestis, and the town Ohrid in North Macedonia with its stunning view of Lake Ohrid, among others. But I never tire of drifting footloose through them. Capua's ruin struck me as something special.

Through arches I could see the surrounding ruins of the baths and likely the ruins of the quarters for the gladiators in training. The arena itself is cleared out, and long, rectangular openings into the rooms below the arena floor have been opened. But the floor itself, with what looks like a circular track around the perimeter that I suspect is used for drainage, is closed to visitors. From a short distance, I could see a sample of the rooms below, where gladiators awaited their time in the arena, or perhaps they were for animals that would become part of the show.

The seating area around the arena has not been restored; cement-like stone, like some sections in Rome's Colosseum, cover what would have been benches. Other seating areas are covered with earth adorned with small bunches of scrub brush. I found myself remembering scenes from the Kirk Douglas film *Spartacus* of the training and the spectacles that would have taken place here. That was a Hollywood set, of course. But the image is clear in my mind as I look out over this arena. Archaeologists still have a lot of exploring and restoration ahead of them.

As usual, I become intrigued by myths surrounding various gods and goddesses. I had never heard of Mithra, and I wished I had asked Antonio more about him. It took some study to understand this mythical creature. He was not a Greek god who was transformed into a Roman god, which was the normal practice. He originated in Indo-Iranian mythology, and his cult was spread by Roman soldiers as far west as England. According to myth, Mithra was born bearing a torch and a knife. He was a child of the earth itself and became the god of light. He killed a sacred bull, and the bull's blood is what fertilizes the earth and allows the growth of vegetation. In this vein, Mithra was often paired with Anahita, a Persian goddess of life-giving water. Ancient Romans often associated her with their goddess Venus.

Christianity was threatening pagan Rome, and soldiers, who had discovered the cult of Mithra in the eastern part of the empire, brought it with them when they returned. Some believe this was done to counteract the Christian influence. After all, the cult survived from the first century to the fourth, when Christianity was allowed to be practiced. A couple of emperors, Commodus and Julian, were practitioners of the cult, and a third, Diocletian, had a temple built on the Danube River in Germany, ostensibly believing its presence would protect the empire.

Roman soldiers and those few emperors made up a lot of those initiated. The rituals were secret. Apparently, there were seven levels of initiation. At one time, ancient texts supposedly were written detailing the cult's secrets, but they have been lost.

The worshiping of this god took place in a temple structure known as a Mithraeum. There apparently were hundreds of these sanctuaries throughout the empire—including the one that still exists in Santa Maria Capua Vetere. I had rambled around the town for a couple of days. I visited the museum, where I would have unknowingly passed a chiseled image of Mithra, the amphitheater, and spent time generally getting acquainted with the town.

I spent one afternoon in modern Capua, just three miles away, admiring the medieval buildings and pleasant squares. This town sits at the junction of the Via Appia and the Via Latina where the roads crossed the river Volturnus (Volturno) on a bridge that still exists. Hannibal and the Romans, in a series of close encounters, traded control of this area during a year or so following Cannae.

On my last day, late in the afternoon, someone in a coffee bar, during a routinely friendly conversation, told me about the

Mithraeum just a few blocks away and only several hundred feet from my rooms. So close, and I had missed it. I found the structure. It had closed for the evening, and I would be gone the next day before it opened.

Later, to understand what I had missed seeing in this restored L-shaped, cavern-like sanctuary, I turned to a book by Maarten Jozef Vermaseren, who apparently wrote tomes on the various Mithraea he visited around Western Europe. I learned that this structure was discovered in 1922, excavated two years later, and that the cavern had been filled with rubble and junk. Originally, folks speculated that Christians in ancient Capua filled the place this way when the cult dispersed and the doors were hammered shut for several centuries. But there was no church built on the site, which was the usual Christian practice of getting rid of pagan temples. They probably were not to blame for the clutter.

Most impressive in this restored sanctuary is the mural on the back wall depicting a beautifully dressed, youthful, powerful Mithra slaying a white buffalo-like bull. A brown dog is pictured in the scene, lapping up the bull's blood; a snake and a scorpion are gripping various parts of the bull's body. The ceiling seemed to represent the heavens. At one time, the stucco was embedded with jewels or bits of colored glass, now long gone. Vermaseren speculates that the brickwork on the walls indicates they were installed during the period of the emperors Trajan and Hadrian. That would have made it sometime between A.D. 98 and 138.

Early the next morning, with caffè and croissant consumed, I begin a slow drive that will take me through the two villages that Strabo described as being along the Via Appia between

ancient Capua and Beneventum: Calatia and Caudium. Calatia appears on modern maps as Maddaloni and is roughly
twelve miles southeast from Santa Maria Capua Vetere. I take
the SS7, passing close to my now-vacated rooms, but quickly
turn off at a point known as Casapulla and move onto the original Via Appia route, now a paved street. From there, I follow
it for the seven miles to Maddaloni. The next town, Montesarchio, known as Caudium when Horace and friends stopped
for a brief visit, is another fourteen miles in a slightly northeast direction. We are now back on the SS7, and Benevento is
still another twelve miles beyond.

I suspect our Roman diplomats would have stopped at
Calatia for the night before pressing on to Cocceius's "well-
stocked villa [overlooking] the inns of Caudium." Horace
does not tell us, of course. Here, before taking off for Beneventum, he provides a satirical bit of entertainment provided by
Sarmentus the jester and his owner, Messius Cicirrus. Sarmentus encourages Messius to "dance a dance of the Cyclo-
pean shepherd." I suspect one would have had to be there
to fully understand the meaning of this small aside. Horace
sums it up nicely: "So we prolonged that supper with all our
laughter."

Quickly, before the morning turned to midday, I reached
Maddaloni. There appeared to be no ruins of the Calatia, just
piles of stones and what I later read was a pre-Roman necropolis. There was a lot of protohistory here, long before the Romans took over. Apparently Calatia was founded by a tribe
known as the Oscans. Another larger group, the Samnites,
battled with them several times, with domination of the town
changing hands through much of the fourth century B.C. It
appears that Julius Caesar, who would have passed through
the village often as a young censor responsible for maintaining

the Via Appia and later as a general leading armies back and forth, established a colony there in 59 B.C. There is a museum, the Museo archeologico di Calatia. As was my usual bad luck, it was closed. I had passed through on a Tuesday, the staff's day off.

I pressed on toward Horace's Caudium. Its modern name, Montesarchio, was likely given to the ancient town during the Middle Ages. This was a quick visit. I knew I would be passing a narrow valley off the Via Appia between two high mountains, Taburno and Traiano, and just before Montesarchio. In that valley, in 321 B.C., the native peoples who controlled the area, the Samnites, tricked the Roman army into going there where they quickly found themselves stymied. Samnites were in front, behind, and above. It is known as the Battle of the Caudine Forks, but it really wasn't a battle. The trapped Romans knew they could not win, and their soldiers soon would face starvation. They surrendered and were allowed to file under a symbolic yoke of raised Samnite spears, adding to their humiliation.

This period in the calendar was before Rome had completely taken over, unifying Italy, and they were doing it slowly, piece by piece. The Samnites had held them off but not for long. In 316 B.C., just five years later, the Romans returned and reversed the circumstances, adding another part of Campania to its republic. By 264 B.C., all of Italy would be under the Roman standard. Eventually, Caudium was destroyed; no one seems to know when or even where it was, specifically. The last time its name appeared in old documents was in the ninth century A.D.

This route of the Via Appia, after passing the valley of the Caudine Forks, makes a big loop for the next twenty miles, heading to the northeast toward Benevento. It then scrapes its way through the heart of the city before dropping down in a southeasterly direction for a few miles toward my lodgings for the next few nights in the tiny village of San Nazzaro. Because the Via Appia entered the Apennine Mountains after leaving Maddalone, it was impossible for the Romans to build a straight road because of high ridges and deep valleys, and the SS7 remains faithful to that long-ago routing.

After reconnecting to the SS7 a short distance outside of San Nazzaro, it shifts southward, dogging it over and around hills all the way to Horace's birthplace, modern Venosa, beyond to the Ionian Sea coast at Taranto and then due east to Brindisi.

I planned to drive into Benevento for a short visit this time through, opting for a much longer stay there on my way back in two months. But for now, the plan was for a couple of days of relaxation in the San Nazzaro countryside. The small village, with barely more than eight hundred Sannazzareni, has only a handful of streets within its two square kilometers. The one that seems to have the most activity sported a pleasant bar with an outdoor terrace. I walked there a couple of times each day for my usual caffè. There were a couple of restaurants nearby for regular meals, and I wanted to spend most of my three days there working in my rooms at B&B La Tartaruga.

Then my host, Antonio Roberto, had a surprise. In casual conversation with my very basic Italian, I had described my project about following the Via Appia. A few hours later, he told me we were meeting a friend of his, Roberto Pellino, a geologist who had studied the Via Appia and knew where its unmarked ancient route was in the countryside around Benevento. Roberto lives in the nearby town of San Giorgio del Sannio, which sits directly on the Via Appia.

We met Roberto Pellino in a small restaurant in his village. Joining us was Maria Grazia Maione, an English speaker who was willing to interpret for us. Over coffee and pastry, Roberto told of two Roman bridges over two different rivers in the area to the south and east of Benevento. One was still intact, the other in grand disarray. He said he would take me there the next day. The main road through San Giorgio del Sannio, which ran past our outdoor table, paved over and automobile laden, was the original Via Appia, now a few feet below the asphalt.

We talked about the Romans and about how Benevento's original names shifted from Malies to Maloenton to Malventum under the Oscans or the Samnites. When the Romans took over, it became Beneventum. It was a delightful hour or so. Maria Grazia had to leave, and Roberto agreed to meet me the next morning a few blocks away in front of his house, which conveniently sat alongside the Via Appia (known locally as the Via Roma).

The next morning Roberto was waiting by the curb. He directed me out of San Giorgio del Sannio on Via Roma, and we continued toward Benevento following the SS7. This, he said, was mostly along the original route. We left it before we reached where it entered the city that had been ruled by the Lombards during the Middle Ages. We swung around to the city's southern edge, near where the ancient Via Appia would have come out after serving as Beneventum's *decumanus maximus,* or main road.

Here, we found our first Roman bridge, the Ponte Leproso, that carried the ancient road over the Sabato River. The name was likely given to the bridge in the early Middle Ages; its original name is believed to have been Marmoreo, although documentation is a bit shaky on this point. It is long and paved, with a slight hump in the middle and what appear to be original stones. No cars are allowed, but walkers and bicyclists were welcome. This bridge is beautifully maintained. It has three large center arches with a smaller arch on each end. The Sabato, a tributary of the Calore River, which hosts the remains of another Roman bridge, is wide and swiftly flowing at this point.

Roberto stopped to talk with a friend, Pasquale, a maintenance worker who was sweeping the curb edges. As they talked, I wandered back and forth across the bridge and down onto the banks below to see the view of the arches, beautifully crafted in brick and stone. It was impressive, almost as impressive as the remains I had seen in Italy of Roman-built viaducts. Reading about it later, I could see that its excellent condition is thanks to good maintenance over the centuries, including rebuilding after earthquakes and destruction by the Goths in the sixth century. Obviously, it was an important crossing point for various peoples over the first millennium A.D.

We moved on. Roberto directed me off the main highways and onto country roads. We started down one, with a Roman house's foundation wall off to one side. This was in the Contrada (District of) Monache, and it rolled up and down small hills buried in heavy woods. A magnificent drive through intense nature. "What is this?" I asked. Roberto smiled. "È la Via Appia," he said. I was astounded. This was not identified as such on any maps I had seen. But Roberto knew. He was friends with archaeologists and other scientists who studied these things. The road was barely wide enough for two cars passing. It was basically a farm road. The presence of the Roman foundation alongside that portion before the deep woods convinced me. We kept going and found another section like the first but adorned with water-filled potholes and muddy stretches. This section eventually joined the provincial road SP28 in the Contrada San Giovanni.

Then we bounced through mud over what could barely pass as a road and found ourselves in Contrada Ponterotto. Roberto said we were only nine miles from Benevento, and the Calore River was nearby. We got out of the car and walked across a soggy field for a few hundred feet. In the middle of the field were the remains of a bridge's arch. It stood very tall and, despite its condition, was in full command of the field below. A short distance away, a remnant of a pier that once was a base for a side of an arch, now long gone, rose against the sky and trees, also in the middle of the field. A couple of columns remained as well. I could see no evidence of a river. Still, we walked and there between the edge of the field and the beginning of a tree line was the sound of water, a mere trickling sound. We stepped down a bank and a small stream, barely flowing, passed under the stone remains of a base that once held an arch. It was obvious that a couple of millennia ago the Calore was a wide, raging river, and the Romans, to carry the Via Appia over it, had to build a high, stunning bridge. It was built in the first century B.C. and was used until the seventh century A.D.

This *ponte rotto*, or ruined bridge, was known as Ponte Appiano, and it still carries that name today. The Via Appia crossed it and dropped down where the far bank would have been, heading up the small hill. Roberto pointed to that spot. Today, there is no evidence that a road went up that hillside. Two farmers' fields sit side by side, divided by a grassy spot about the width of what the Roman road would be. It was tempting to want to walk up that hillside, knowing the original

Via Appia was just a few feet below. But the mud would have made it tough going.

This spot is between Benevento, just nine miles away, and the now long-gone ancient town of Aeclanum, fewer than five miles away. It is now in the modern town of Mirabella Eclano. We drove to the archaeological site but were turned away by a couple sitting at the closed gate. This was during the Covid-19 pandemic, and despite our masks and promises to only go in for a quick look, the area was closed. They did not know when it would reopen.

That day with Roberto was a highlight of my trip. Without him, I never would have found those stretches of hidden—at least to the casual traveler—pathways through farmers' fields with handfuls of scattered Roman ruins alongside. We drove back to San Giorgio del Sannio, I dropped him at his home along the Via Appia / Via Roma, and I returned to San Nazzaro, the friendly coffee bar with its comfortable outdoor terrace, and sat in the cool of the late September evening.

I had another journey to plan. Unlike Horace and his friends, I would remain on the Via Appia route from Benevento due south, staying for a few days in Venosa, then Taranto, and then the end of the road at Brindisi, which would end up being a major highlight of my three months of travel. Horace, et al., jumped off the Via Appia at Beneventum and headed southeast to the Adriatic coast to reach Brundisium on a series of dirt pathways that still had nearly 150 years to go before Emperor Trajan would order a new Roman road to be built. This would be the route I would take near the end of my journey when I would head back to Rome. But first, a few nights in Horace's birthplace, Venosa.

8

A VERY SHORT RIVER

Antonius [Mark Antony] *had been lured on by the treaties of Tarentum and Brundisium, and by his marriage with the sister* [of Octavian], *and paid by his death the penalty of a treacherous alliance* [with Cleopatra]. *No doubt, there was peace after all this, but it was a peace stained with blood.*
——Roman historian Publius Cornelius Tacitus

H orace and friends move on toward Brundisium the day after that strange evening in the villa overlooking the "inns of Caudium." Sarmentus, freedman to Maecenas, was along on the journey.

In typical fashion, our poet/diplomat gives a quick nod to Beneventum. All he says is that "our busy host nearly burned the inn turning lean thrushes over the fire. . . . You saw scared servants and famished guests snatch food and everyone tried to extinguish the roaring blaze." That's it for Beneventum, which would have been one of the larger villages in that part of south-central Italy. The offering of "lean thrushes" likely indicates the inn was modest and not quite like the luxurious villas of friends and magistrates to which they had become accustomed.

Here, we lose track. At some point southeast of Beneventum, after crossing the now-shattered bridge over the Calore River and beyond the ancient village of Aeclanum, the travelers leave the Via Appia, likely at what Horace identifies as "a villa near Trivicum" where they spend a frustrating night, at least for Horace. The *Barrington Atlas* places this spot with a question mark next to the name just a few miles off the fabled roadway and probably a day's journey from Beneventum. No one really knows for sure where that spot is. The pack of diplomats, after experiencing another smoky dinner because the fuel for the fire was "green wood, foliage and all," settled in, but Horace admits to seeking sex from a young woman who does not show up: "Here like an utter fool I lay wakeful till midnight awaiting a cheating girl." One wonders what kind of villa this distinguished cluster of men chose for their lodging.

Their precise route now becomes a mystery. They are still in the Apennine Mountains, but from Trivicum they could easily have traveled through various river valleys headed toward the sea on a route that, in the empire's second century, became the Via Aurelia Aeclanensis. We only know that from the smoky villa, they rush on "in a cart twenty-four miles to spend the night in a little town I can't fit in the verse."

At one time, some classicists speculated that this town, unnamable, was Horace's birthplace of Venusia. This is not likely; it is well beyond twenty-four Roman miles. He mentions that those in the unmentionable town sell water that is usually free elsewhere, but "the bread's the best by far." So, they load up on that staple and head for the Adriatic coast, likely joining up with what was then known as the Via Minucia, whose name comes from the Greek meaning "mule track." This roadway, scoured out of the rocky soil in 125 B.C., was paved over at the personal expense of Emperor Trajan more than two hundred years later. It was renamed Via Traiana in his honor.

Horace and his colleagues are now well off the Queen of Roads and heading southeast to the coast. Their new route, once they leave the mountains behind, will take them along flat coastal land and save them a day's journey to Brundisium. I will follow that final segment of their journey later during my return trip to Rome, eventually heading north and then west from Brindisi, through Bari and Troia, and back to Benevento.

But for now, as I head to Brindisi, I choose to stay on the hillier Via Appia. Some of its precise route is guessed at in *Barrington*. But SS7 will likely get me on some portions of the original route as I travel sixty-nine miles from San Nazzaro to my next lodgings in Venosa. Horace knew it by the Latin name Venusia and apparently had warm feelings toward it, mentioning it in some of his poetry:

> *So that, however the east wind might threaten the Italian*
> *waves, thrashing the Venusian woods,*
> *you'll be safe, yourself, and rich rewards will flow from*
> *the source,*
> *from even-handed Jupiter, and from*
> *Neptune*

I am staying in a hotel in Venosa, the Hotel Villa del Sorriso, located on what I discovered was the Via Appia route. It is not the SS7. It is a provincial road, SP10, which is identified by street signs in the town as the Via Appia. The SS7, farther to the north, immediately turns south near San Nazzaro and drifts away from the original route by a handful of miles to the west. When it crosses the line from Campania into Basilicata, the modern road spends much of its time wandering away from the old road route, nearly all the way to the Ionian Sea. The *Barrington Atlas* shows the road passing through the town of Aquilonia near Beneventum, then gently sweeping southeast toward Venusia. Aquilonia today is known as Lacedonia.

But the original roadway has been hard to find. When the Via Traiana was built more than four hundred years after the Via Appia, that route became the favored line of travel to the port city of Brundisium. The Via Appia south of Beneventum, in large part, was abandoned, which makes its stony remains—now buried deep beneath farmers' fields, olive groves, and vineyards— hard to uncover in the modern world.

I learned that it is important for the traveler in search of the roadway to pay attention to *Barrington* and not be lulled into the easy glide along SS7, which had been so loyal to its ancestor up to this point. Here, far from the SS7, I entered Venosa on that provincial road that felt right to follow as I neared the town. And just before I reached my hotel, my iPhone gives its address on the Via Appia.

One thing was encouraging. SP10 runs to the heart of Venosa, marked by a four-way roundabout, and transforms into SP18, which quickly reaches the archaeological park and the known ruins of Venusia on the other side of town. It is conceivable that the original road over which I entered ran straight through what then would have been countryside and reached the village.

The archaeological site is not large. In addition to ruins of stone walls, it has, nearby, a partially buried circular Roman amphitheater that long ago could hold ten thousand spectators. I could see, walking the perimeter, a long road paved in the Roman style running through a portion of it. That stretch in the ruins was in almost a direct line with SP10/Via Appia and SP18/Via Roma. I felt sure that I had not lost my way.

Venosa is a comfortable town, not beautiful but quite functional looking with significant postwar development. What makes it an attractive visit is its beautifully restored medieval center. It is a living display of ancient fragments, mounted to architecturally pleasing structures put up long after the Romans left. The streets, fountains, churches, and palazzo feature blocks of stone that, as someone described, bear traces of "the Roman chisel." There is a scattering of brick structures that go back more than two thousand years.

And among buildings from a much later era, on a side street paved with a stunning array of cobblestones, there is a lovely brick structure dating back to Roman times. It is supposedly the house of Horace. Reading about Venosa and its connection with Horace before my visit, I had discovered that researchers, sometime after the mid-twentieth century, determined that this building was part of a private bath complex built in the first century A.D. Since Horace was born in Venusia in 65 B.C., his family home obviously was elsewhere. Where? No one knows, of course. In the ruins of the ancient village to the east of the modern town are remains of a handful of Roman houses. Perhaps there? We will probably never know, at least until future archaeologists uncover a stone with the name Flaccus, Horace's surname, carved on it.

Townspeople for a millennium or two, proud of the fact that the famous poet was born here and wrote lovingly about the countryside and its deep woods, needed something physical to identify his presence. At some point between then and now, some enterprising townsperson decided to capitalize on his presence to draw tourists and classical scholars.

The "house" was open. A tall, friendly looking man sat at its doorway smoking. He invited me in. It did not look like a house at all. There were no interior rooms, just a large space that would better fit a Roman bath than a family abode. There were souvenirs for sale and lots of books on many subjects, all in Italian. There were no pamphlets about the place in English. The host was apologetic. More Americans are visiting, he said, adding that the tourist office should publish information in different languages. I spent a pleasant hour thumbing through this and that and had a nice conversation, struggling in my basic Italian, with the gentleman. I did not challenge him on whether this was Horace's childhood home. It simply was not important. What was important were his remarks about the late-nineteenth-century statue of Horace in the middle of the medieval square, the Piazza Orazio Flacco. It depicts a tall, imposing Orazio, Italian for Horace. The poet had described himself as rather short and not too regal. We talked about how the statue is simply a representation of the man whose appearance and features must simply have been a guess.

Contributing to the belief that Horace would have been raised elsewhere is the knowledge that his father, whom he worshiped, was an Italian freedman and possible landowner who lost that land and was enslaved around 90 B.C., when towns in the area revolted against Roman domination. When the Romans took back their control, three thousand Venusians were enslaved and lost their lands. His father could have been one of them and might later have been granted freedom—hence becoming a freedman whose land was not returned to him.

But with a doting father—Horace never mentions his mother in any of his writings—he somehow manages to be educated in Rome. According to an article from the Chicago-based Poetry Foundation, "Horace was fifteen (and surely in Rome) when Caesar's army crossed the Rubicon," initiating a civil war in 49 B.C. "While Horace studied, Caesar battled Pompey [46 B.C.].... Horace was in Athens when Caesar was assassinated [44 B.C.]." And most interesting, a very young Horace left his studies in Athens to join the army of one of Caesar's assassins, Marcus Brutus. In his writings, Horace claimed he was at Philippi in Macedonia, today's Northern Greece, and said he threw away his shield in panic and ran from the battlefield. Some literary scholars believe Horace embellished his role at Philippi. If embellished, it certainly was poetic:

I was there at Philippi, with you, in that
headlong flight, sadly leaving my shield behind,
when shattered Virtue, and what threatened
from an ignoble purpose, fell to earth.

But he did return to Rome after Mark Antony and Octavian defeated Brutus and the other assassin, Cassius. The victors granted amnesty to those who had fought against them, and in a few years Horace, now a friend of the future emperor, was traveling in a diplomatic party along the Via Appia and then to the Adriatic coast and on to Brundisium and Tarentum to help patch things up between two of Rome's most towering figures near the death of the republic and the birth of empire.

Ancient Venusia was important as a Roman military center for many years. In fact, Octavian rewarded soldiers from one of his victorious legions by settling them here, granting them land. But that militaristic role shifted as Rome gained control of all Southern Italy. The town's commercial success, spurred by the presence of the Via Appia over a couple of centuries, diminished when that stretch south of Beneventum was supplanted by the Via Traiana to the east. In fact, all Roman Apulia, today's

Puglia region, declined during the late empire. It became part of the Byzantine Empire, sometimes referred to as the Eastern Roman Empire, by around 450. That is when the Western Roman Empire, ultimately ruled from Ravenna when Rome fell, declined in power. While some towns were depopulated, Bari and Brindisi grew as Byzantine centers.

Most of my few days in Venosa were spent simply wandering the town, passing Horace's statue more than once and ambling down that delightful cobblestone street in front of the knockoff known as the house of Horace, admiring it not as his abode but for its wonderful restoration as a solid reminder of Roman times. The medieval center is well preserved and, while not big, it is easy for a wanderer to get lost in history. Eventually it was time to move on toward Taranto where, twenty-three years earlier, I had spent a week on another journey through the past. It was there I had first met Horace, and I was looking forward to doing it again.

The *Barrington Atlas* shows dotted lines that represent estimates of the route of the Via Appia, from Venusia to the ancient village of Silvium (modern Gravina in Puglia). From there, the line turns solid, showing the known route. It heads south and slightly east before slipping around the city of Matera, which did not exist in Roman times, and running directly into Tarentum (modern Taranto).

I followed as closely as possible and from Gravina, using two connecting provincial roads, SP53 and SP6 to the northern edge of Matera where I rejoined the SS7, with encouraging signs identifying it as Via Appia, straight south to Taranto. That coastal city was where Horace and his party would end up in 37 B.C. They had turned west toward Tarentum, forty-four miles away, after arriving at Brundisium at the end of that coastal route then known as the Via Minucia.

Interestingly, Horace does not mention ending up at the treaty negotiations at that delightful port city on the Ionian Sea. He ends his satire simply by saying, "[Brundisium's] the end of a long road and this story." After all, we must remember that Horace was a poet and storyteller, not a historian. And we need to read his satire with the understanding that the real trip was embellished with a bit of fiction. He wrote nothing about what he and Virgil and the other dignitaries in his party did during the renegotiations of the original Treaty of Brundisium, turning it into the Treaty of Tarentum.

Basically, the earlier pact between Octavian and Mark Antony was fraying a bit. We must remember that the pair, along with another Roman, the general Lepidus, had, after Caesar's murder, formed a triumvirate to rule the soon-to-be-empire: Octavian controlled the west, Antony the east, and Lepidus ruled North Africa. But Octavian had problems with another general, Sextus Pompeius, the younger son of Pompey whom Caesar defeated a decade earlier. Sextus was bent on revenge over Caesar's inheritors. Octavian needed help, and he turned to Antony. The pair and their delegates met in Tarentum to recast their pact; this new treaty would last for five years.

Under the agreement, Antony would provide Octavian with ships with which to battle Sextus, and Octavian would give Antony troops for his expected battle in the east with the Parthians, a people who occupied a part of what today is Iran. Antony kept his word. Octavian got his ships and an eventual victory over Sextus. But Antony never got the promised additional legions, and the following year he was badly defeated in that faraway land of Parthia. Octavian, later as Augustus, ironically made peace with those former enemies.

So by 31 B.C., the knot that held Octavian and Antony together irredeemably began to unravel. Octavian knew war was inevitable. He did not want it to be a civil war with a fellow Roman, so he declared war against Egypt, not Antony. This made Cleopatra the target. Their Egyptian fleet sailed to the Greek coastline on the Adriatic at a place known as Actium and, on September 2 that year, met Octavian's fleet, controlled by the future ruler's best friend from childhood, Marcus Agrippa. Agrippa won in the name of Octavian. Antony and Cleopatra limped back to Alexandria, Egypt. In August the following year, as Octavian's forces reached Egypt, they committed their famous suicides. Three years later, in 27 B.C., Octavian, with Antony and Lepidus out of the way, was named Caesar Augustus, and the Roman Republic, which had lasted 482 years, was devoured by the new empire. The Western Roman Empire lasted a bit longer than its predecessor: 503 years. The Eastern Roman Empire, primarily under the Byzantines, lasted the longest: 1,168 years, ending in 1453 when the Muslims conquered Constantinople, today's Istanbul.

The drive south from Matera is one of my favorite stretches of the Via Appia. It is mostly straight, with the first handful of miles heading southeast. Then, after a gentle turn southward, the car glides smoothly through a mostly flat countryside. When I first drove it more than two decades earlier, it had a fresh coat of well-laid asphalt, and I remember almost no traffic. The pace of vehicles might have picked up more in the intervening years, but it was still mostly free of heavy trucks and high-speed Italian drivers. During my four days in Taranto on this trip, I traveled that stretch twice simply to enjoy the sights of the land and to rediscover the kind of straight stretch that Roman roadbuilders preferred.

Approaching Taranto from the north is a straight-on affair. Just before Via Appia/SS7 reaches the edge of the city's bay, known as the Little Sea, it turns east, toward Brindisi. I pass up that turn, and in a few moments I am on the bridge that connects the northern coastline to a long narrow island that once held the Roman town with origins way back beyond Rome—and is now lost in the mists of time. Only in those days, it was not an island. It was a peninsula joined to the land along the inside of the heel of Italy's boot, dividing the grand Ionian Sea from the natural harbor known as the Little Sea. Today, on the opposite end of the island, there is another bridge, which takes the traveler into the port city of Taranto. After driving the length of the island (which sadly exhibits only modernized medieval structures that replaced the Roman buildings hundreds of years ago) and passing a small plot with a scattering of classical ruins dating back to the Greeks, I cross the second bridge and find my rooms a few blocks away. The city seems a bit more frenetic and crowded than I remember from that first visit, but it is full of nice shops and good restaurants. Many streets are pedestrian only, and that made for a pleasant stroll after *la cena,* my evening meal.

I looked for and found a bench near the center of a park between my rooms and the south bridge. This bridge connects the mainland to the former peninsula that was severed and turned into the island in A.D. 480, during the Middle Ages. The bench, unoccupied, was the same one I had relaxed on years earlier. I sat, smoked a short Toscanello cigar, and refreshed my memory of what I had learned about Horace then and connected it to what I know now.

We do not have an accounting of any role he played during those negotiations between Octavian and Mark Antony for their new treaty. Perhaps he was just along for the ride, out of his friendship with the likes of Virgil, Maecenas, Cocceius, and Fonteius Capito. He did write about Tarentum in his *Second Book of Odes:* 6, "Tibur and Tarentum." I read it long ago and reread it on this late September evening, with the sounds of laughter from young adults gathered around a cluster of nearby benches and the pleasant yells of youngsters kicking a soccer ball, nonstop. It was a wonderful dusky setting for a gratifying fall evening.

Horace, during that visit or perhaps during several other journeys along the Via Appia, had passed through Tarentum, which he lovingly writes about in his ode. In it, he discusses places he would like to live in old age, "when I am tired of the seas, and the roads, and all the endless fighting." He mentions "Tibur, founded by men of Greece" as his first choice. Tibur is today's Tivoli, a place east of Rome where emperors after Horace's time built fabulous estates. It must have been a pleasant village before the very rich and powerful took it over. But Horace writes in his ode, "If the cruel Fates deny me that place, I will head for the river Galaesus, sweet with its precious sheep, on Spartan fields."

The river Galaesus, now called Galeso, is a short, stubby river that rises out of a marshland and runs for less than a mile to the Little Sea. During that visit several years before—and intrigued by Horace's description of this short river—I had asked a cabdriver for directions. He took me there and stayed awhile, telling me the story of how Allied bombing during World War II had pummeled the area around the river and a naval station along the Little Sea's shoreline.

We parted on a small bridge over the river, full of fish feeding in an eddy below. I slowly walked along a pathway on the bank, in what I imagined were Horace's footsteps, to the Little Sea where fishermen tied up their boats. It certainly was not as glorious as Horace remembered with its flocks of precious sheep. Now on this twenty-first-century journey, armed with a car, I decided to drive there the next day, confident I would remember the route around the Little Sea's northern edge.

Early the next morning, I found a nearby coffee shop on the edge of that leafy park and ordered two double espressos in a row, consuming far more coffee that any decent Italian would. The waiter, sensing I had a greater need for early morning caffeine that his usual customers, politely asked, in excellent English, "Would you prefer an Americano?" This was a drink created for tourists where they simply fill a larger espresso cup with hot water and mix it with an ordinary small espresso shot. "Please, no," I said. "I need it to be stronger." Later, he asked if I wanted a third. "No, thank you. Two is enough." It was a glorious morning, not hot and perfectly comfortable. A peaceful moment that lingers in my memory.

The drive across the island and onto the mainland to the north took me directly to a small street that seemed to head in the right direction around the edge of the Little Sea. The sign said the road, lined by shops and a few restaurants, was the Via Galeso. I suspected I was on the right track. A few moments later, I saw a small dirt road with a hand-painted sign nailed to a tree and an arrow. It said: FIUME GALESO. Moments later, I was standing on the spot where the taxi driver had dropped me off years earlier. The bridge he had driven over was gone. In its place was a weathered wooden stairway and small walkway that took folks on foot from one side to the other. Or on bicycles. Just as I was letting this change sink in, two men in tight-fitting bicyclist regalia rode up, dismounted, picked up their bikes and headed up the steps of the small bridge to the other side, a few feet away. The dirt road is now a walking and bicycle path. The men waved goodbye and were gone.

The Galeso certainly is not wide, perhaps ten or twelve feet. I looked toward its origins, several dozen feet away in a marsh or swamp, and then turned back toward the Little Sea, less than a mile away. But there were other differences as well. The path along the bank toward the sea, which Horace would have walked more than two thousand years ago and that I had traversed, is still there. But vegetation has taken over. The path was blocked by huge mounds of riverside bushes. I made it a few dozen feet, but it was clear this was not a regular walking path and authorities felt they had no need to keep it clear.

I stopped, walked back to my car parked across a wide field where I imagined Horace's "precious sheep" had once pastured, and decided I would carry the memory of my earlier visit. This is now an industrial area, and a large nursery filled with trees and surrounded by ugly wire fencing of some sort bumps up to the river. The elevated, traffic-filled SS7 toward Brindisi blasts over it, along with a railroad bridge high above the wooden walkway. Once, when the ancient Via Appia was grounded here (now buried below the modern SS7), there must have been a small Roman bridge made of bricks and stone.

I sat and read Horace's ode one more time, focusing on what he wrote about this once-glorious spot: "That corner of earth is the brightest to me, where the honey gives nothing away to that of Hymettus." He was saying the honey harvested along this river was at least equal to the famous honey harvested on the slopes of Mount Hymettus, near Athens, Greece.

The modern city of Taranto long ago spread well beyond the ancient village on what is now an island. There might have been colonists from Crete mingling here with a local tribe. Some classicists interpret myths to say Taranto got its name from Taras, son of Poseidon, god of seas and waters. Apparently, Taras was shipwrecked, and his father sent a dolphin to carry him to safety. The spot he landed, the peninsula-now-island, is where he founded Tarentum.

Then came the Romans who, after a long struggle with powerful forces, took over in 272 B.C. When Hannibal showed up in 212 B.C., the city sided with him against the Romans. But they got it back five years later. The people were punished for their disloyalty, and slowly over the next century Tarentum recovered its wealth and leisurely life. It became a favorite of Augustus and, eventually, a Roman colony.

After my visit to the river, I spent the rest of my three days sitting on my bench in the park reading history and trying to understand many of the characters that came and went over two thousand years. Modern Taranto is a nice place in which to settle, take a break from a long journey, and contemplate. The streets are safe, the restaurants are many, and my regular server at the morning coffee shop is delightful and full of life.

Now, I am near the end of that famous Roman road that has witnessed so much. Brindisi, just forty-four miles to the east, is where the road met the sea. And when it was called Brundisium, it was the gateway to the Roman east. I was scheduled to spend a week there before moving across the Adriatic to explore that part of the story. What clues can Brindisi give me and is it possible to walk along a short section of the Via Appia outside the city gate that still stands? That is what Cicero did with Julius Caesar when the victorious general forgave Cicero for supporting Pompey in one of the greatest civil wars in Roman history.

9

BRINDISI

Next day the weather was better, the road was worse,
Right up to fishy Barium [modern Bari].
Then Gnatia, on whose building
The water-nymphs frowned, brought
us laughter and mirth,
As it tried to persuade us that incense melts without fire
On its temple steps.

—Horace

Horace's satire speeds up, again carrying the reader over long distances in few words. After Trivicum, where he failed to share his bed with a young woman who did not show up as promised, his party goes to Canusium, today known as Canosa, which is fewer than one hundred miles due east from Benevento and off the eastern slope of the Apennine Mountains. The poet tells us that the town was founded by "brave Diomedes," a Greek hero of the Trojan War who may or may not have existed. He warns his reader that the bread there was gritty, and water was scarce. And he mentions that their traveling companion, Varius, "peels off, to the grief of his weeping friends." Why did Varius leave, and where did he go? Horace offers no clue.

It was at Canusium, in 209 B.C., more than 180 years before Horace's journey, where the Romans battled Hannibal and his Carthaginians. It was a three-day fight, neither side won, and losses were high. Some fourteen thousand men from both sides were killed.

Hannibal, as we know, spent fifteen years in Italy, extracting heavy tolls that resulted in the deaths of tens of thousands of Romans. Following his victory at Cannae, in 216 B.C., where his army of forty thousand infantry and ten thousand calvary is thought to have killed as many as seventy thousand Romans out of a force of eighty thousand in one afternoon, legend has it that he was urged by his commander of calvary, Maharbal, to besiege Rome. Hannibal declined, preferring to stay in Southern Italy. According to the historian Livy, a disappointed Maharbal told him, "You know, Hannibal, how to win a fight; you do not know how to use your victory."

If Hannibal had gone to the gates of Rome as Maharbal urged and been successful, Rome would have been finished. The Mediterranean would have been a Carthaginian lake instead of a Roman one. I have often wondered what that would have done to the Western European history we know so well. Some authors believe in revisionist theory that Carthaginian motivation in opposing Rome was commercial trading and not conquest, and that defeat of Rome would not have changed much in the course of Western history. But that would not happen. Historian Patrick Hunt, writing for *Britannica,* says this of Rome's brutal defeat at Cannae: "In spite of the massive blow to Rome's morale and its manpower in the short term, Cannae ultimately steeled Roman resistance for the long fight ahead." The Romans rebuilt their legions and a succession of generals were able to chip away over the next thirteen years at the Carthaginians' force. Hannibal was unable to repeat the magnitude of his brutal win at Cannae. The Romans eventually drove him back to Carthage in 203 B.C., and legions, led by Scipio Africanus the Elder, defeated him on a battlefield near Carthage just one year later, ending the Second Punic War.

Now I'm on the final leg of the Via Appia, following on the SS7 over much of the original route, leaving Taranto behind and heading toward Brindisi. This section was finished in 191 B.C., the end of a 350-mile project that had begun under the guidance of Appius Claudius Caecus in 312, representing 121 years. It gave Rome, in the final two centuries of the republic and 164 years before Octavian declared himself emperor, a quick, efficient route to move armies from Rome across the Adriatic Sea and on to that other great road, the Via Egnatia. Crossing the Balkans, as historian Bettany Hughes writes, this extension to the Via Appia "would nourish the Roman desire to enjoy an empire without limits." It would lead Rome to the Eastern Silk Roads.

The distance that likely took two days for Horace and his party to reach Taranto took me about an hour to reach Brindisi. I am eastbound; Horace and his companions turned westbound, after arriving in what was then Brundisium along the coastal route that much later became the Via Traiana. I would eventually, in my extended time in the port city, travel up the coast toward Bari and beyond to see what is left of the Via Traiana, but today I needed to find my rooms on the edge of Brindisi's historic center.

The city map is precise and clearly shows the route's pathway into and through the city. When the SS7 crosses a semi-ring road on the outskirts, it flows directly onto a city street named Via Appia. It heads straight as an arrow over several blocks to the spot where the Romans first built a classic gate through the city's ramparts. It was near this *porta* (gate) where the Via Traiana blended into the Via Appia. From the gate and inside the walls, it headed straight to the water's edge, several blocks away. Today, that route inside the historic center is covered by three connecting streets: the Via Carmine, the Via Filomeno Consiglio, and, close to the port, a narrow walkway along Piazza Vittorio Emanuele II.

That gate retains the ancient name Porta Mesagne. It was here that Mark Antony, feuding with his early partner Octavian—allies when they defeated Caesar's murderers at Philippi in Northern Greece—had a moat constructed in front of the Roman gate to aid in his army's siege of the city whose residents had remained loyal to Octavian. They eventually reconciled, hence the two treaties reached at Brundisium and Tarantum. No trace of the moat remains, but the gate and the remains of those ramparts were dramatically renovated as late as the mid-thirteenth century when the medieval Holy Roman emperor Frederick II ordered it done. He wanted an enlarged arch to make a more impressive entry into the city. It was remodeled closer to its size and appearance today in the mid-1500s. At some point, it was renamed Porta Napoli. Later, the original name, which locals probably preferred over the Spanish reference to Naples, was returned. That large, single arch needed a companion next to it, a smaller archway to get pedestrians out of the way of traffic. It was cut through the rampart in the 1930s.

This was all I knew about this part of the city before arriving in late September. For now, during afternoon rush hour traffic, cars and small trucks from three directions were lined up to take turns going through the single-lane arch. I proceeded and turned left, heading to my rooms on a side street just a half block from the remains of a section of the walls.

My plan for the next day was to walk back to the gate and wander along the Via Appia for several blocks heading west. I imagined that this is where Caesar, with his army behind him, dismounted from his horse and met a very nervous Cicero. The Roman philosopher and erstwhile supporter of Caesar's enemy, Pompey—now defeated, disgraced, and on the run— feared death at Caesar's hand. His nervousness was short-lived. Historian Philip Freeman says the pair "continued down the Appian Way in conversation for several miles, walking side by side as the rest of Caesar's party followed behind." Caesar forgave the philosopher, whom he had long known during times of good and ill, and invited him to Rome. They would never be the best of friends, but they needed each other. There would be no banishment. This time.

Reading about what transpired between the two Romans in several Caesar biographies was what first drew me to Brindisi. I did not anticipate the pleasant surprise I would experience meeting, by pure luck, the next day after my walk, an authority on the archaeology of this city and the surrounding area— someone who was willing to spend time over the next five days showing me wonderful things.

I got to my rooms much earlier than I had told my host I would arrive. He was not there to let me in. I wanted to call him, but my cell had no signal. I parked in a forbidden spot in front of his building—nothing else was available—and walked a few blocks to Via Carmine to look for a friendly businessperson who might let me use their store telephone.

Ahead was a dress shop. Inside were a middle-aged woman

and her elderly mother. I told them in my best basic Italian my plight. The mother, with a smile and nodding yes, pointed to their phone. I called my host. He said he would meet me in ten minutes. It was urgent because I could not legally park on his street, and my car was sitting in a spot within a zone for residents only. He said he would help me find parking. On each of the next five days I would walk past the women's dress shop, they would see me, and we would wave. On my last day, I took cornetti and caffè to them. Truly kind, helpful Southern Italians.

The walk early the next morning was uneventful. I strolled the few blocks to the Porta Mesagne, passed through the pedestrian arch, wove around the traffic lining up to enter the historic center, dodged a husband and wife arguing loudly in the tunnel that went under the railroad tracks bringing trains into the adjacent station, came out the other side, and took the most obvious route due west. I passed a modern high-rise apartment building that I later discovered was on the site of the Roman amphitheater, now completely gone, and trudged for perhaps a quarter mile down an ordinary city street. Somewhere along here, Caesar—who would be killed three or four years later—had met and forgiven Cicero, who himself would be killed five years after the dictator. But in that long-ago moment, all was good, all forgiven.

I stopped at some point, looked west, turned, looked east, then sat at a bar's outdoor table and ordered a double caffè. It was ten o'clock. I was done trying to tread in the footsteps of two ancient Romans. It was time to head back to the Porta Mesagne, walk that straight stretch to the port, then visit the archaeological museum and see what I could learn.

This latter stretch, all within Brindisi's historic center, was far more pleasurable than the section outside of the Porta Mesagne. There are shops along those three streets, but there also are low-rise homes carved out of medieval structures, a couple of *farmacie* (pharmacies), and a sprinkling of restaurants. The character of these formerly medieval buildings certainly beat the postwar construction outside of the ramparts.

When I reached the water, I found a convenient bench and sat looking beyond the narrow natural channel, shaped like deer antlers, that fed the Adriatic to the inner harbor. Out there, in the distance perhaps one hundred miles away, was the coast of Albania. When the Romans were here where I was sitting this was, of course, Brundisium. But it had an earlier, slightly different name. The Greek geographer Strabo wrote that one of the old spellings, in the language of the Messapian founders, was Brentesium, which means stag's head. This likely was a reference to the antler-shaped inner harbor.

My mind went back to what happened here after Caesar, in 49 B.C., crossed the Rubicon River into Italy, near today's Rimini, uttering those famous words *alea iacta est* (the die is cast). Or, according to Plutarch, he said it in Greek not Latin. Either way, it triggered a civil war between him and the senate and Pompey, his former friend (and onetime son-in-law). The senate, at Pompey's urging, had ordered Caesar to give up his armies and provinces. If he did not follow those orders, he would be declared an enemy of the state. Caesar refused and marched against Rome. Brundisium played a significant role in all this saber rattling around the spot where I was sitting, enjoying a Toscanello cigar and listening to the scattered sounds from a restaurant and its patrons several feet behind me.

At some point, just three months after Caesar had crossed the Rubicon, Pompey wanted to head to Greece along the Via

Egnatia, where he could build a bigger army from legions stationed in there. To do that, his soldiers needed to take ships from this port. In fact, many senators and other government leaders—temporarily abandoning Rome—had already set sail from here. Caesar knew Pompey and his army would do the same. He was trying to reach Brundisium first to cut him off. He and his legions were skirting the coast along the Adriatic Sea from the north; Pompey was racing down the Via Appia along Italy's western edge. He beat Caesar into the well-fortified city.

As Freeman wrote, "When Caesar reached the port a few days later, he could only watch in frustration as Pompey's men looked down on him from the high stone walls." Caesar surrounded the town on all sides except the area open to the port. Half of Pompey's force had already left for Greece, sailing through the narrow channel that resembles a stag's antlers and out to the open sea. The other half remained, likely encamped around where I was sitting, waiting for the ships to return and carry them eastward. Caesar tried to blockade the channel, building flimsy towers on rafts from which to drop fiery missiles on any troop ships trying to escape.

Pompey—a weak politician but a competent general—commandeered local merchant ships to help break down the blockade. This and other measures eventually led Pompey and his remaining army to blast through Caesar's best efforts at a blockade and make a break across the Adriatic. With no ships available to make a pursuit, Caesar backed off and turned his attentions toward Hispania, today's Spain and Portugal. Pompey had armies there that were loyal to him, and Caesar wanted to stop them from rendezvousing with Pompey in the east.

Says Freeman, "Caesar was now the ruler of Italy, but it was

an empty victory. . . . With the whole Roman government ab-
sconded to Greece, he was just another rebel." Of course, this
"rebel" eventually won. Pompey was defeated the following
year, 48 B.C., at Pharsalus (near modern Fársala) in Central
Greece. Historians today debate the precise location of the battle, but its name, the Battle of Pharsalus, stands. Caesar, by 45
B.C., had mopped up what was left of Pompey's loyalists and
was unchallenged as dictator, moving toward becoming the
first emperor. But the following year, on the Ides of March, that
all ended.

The cool interior of the archaeological museum, from the soft-
hued small courtyard at the entrance that, according to popular
belief, is dedicated to the Order of Saint John of Jerusalem, offered a pleasant diversion after my morning trek along the Via
Appia route to the sea. Two museum employees, sitting behind
a large counter, handed over my ticket. I asked if they knew a
local guide, well versed in history, who could introduce Brindisi
to me. The two conversed quietly for a moment, then said, "Daniele Vitale would be good. We can call him for you."

Excellent! The museum workers called Daniele, told him
about my question, and handed me the phone. He spoke perfect English. He offered to meet me the next day on the small,
narrow street outside my rooms. We should plan on two hours,
he said.

This museum visit was one of the best of my long journey. It
was not huge, like the national museum in Naples, but rather
midsized, well laid out, and nicely appointed with the appropriate ancient and medieval statues and glass cases full of restored Greek and Roman pottery, coins, and tools. I enjoyed it
all. Then I got to the top floor and was dazzled by displays of

the bronzes of Punta del Serrone, recovered in 1992 from the bottom of the Adriatic, about two miles north of Brindisi. This was an incredible find. The display holds about two hundred pieces and includes two male busts dating to the early Roman Empire; bearded heads of two fourth-century Greeks, retaining the likely appearance generally given to philosophers; a partial bust; and two female heads.

Why were they at the bottom of the Adriatic, just off the coast? The explanation, I later found on a Neapolitan site, Life, Death & Miracles, was speculative. Because no ship wreckage was discovered around the submerged bronzes, the writer says that historians guess that they may have been considered defective or inferior and were being sent to a Brindisi foundry to be melted down and recycled. To the modern eye, educated even slightly in ancient history, they certainly are not "inferior." Whoever created these pieces originally in the early days of empire was an artisan of the highest order. And the restoration in the late 1990s and beyond—largely conducted in a special museum lab and in Florence far to the north—equally shows outstanding craftmanship. I visited the museum three times during my five days there; the third time was spent almost exclusively in the top-floor room admiring those masterpieces.

The next morning, as promised, Daniele—who prefers being called Danny—was waiting. After introductions were made, we walked a few hundred feet to the remnants of the city's landside wall. These were not Roman but rather medieval ramparts. They must have been higher at some point. To qualify as "ramparts" they usually would have a walkway higher up for sentries. But Danny, who I discovered possesses a vast knowledge of ancient history and archaeology, told me about what was around this spot in Brindisi's historic center and around Porta Mesagne perhaps a hundred meters or so away. There would have been a theater, amphitheater, temples, and public buildings all around us, with traces of ruins periodically popping up during construction projects.

He said ancient sources indicate that an arch to Emperor Trajan, who ordered the Via Traiana built, was likely once around here but now is gone. That would have been one of at least three arches to Trajan that I knew about. There is one in Mérida, Spain, that was either dedicated to Trajan or simply was the entrance to the temple of my favorite goddess, Diana. Later in my journey, I would see Trajan's arch in Benevento, which was built at the start of the Via Traiana where it breaks off from the Via Appia. I learned there also is one in Ancona, on the Adriatic northeast of Rome. This emperor was quite the builder. He also is remembered in Rome for his huge marketplace next to the Forum and for a tall column with carvings in marble of soldiers, horses, carts, and countryside winding their way up. It tells the story of Trajan's victory over the Dacians, a people based on the Black Sea along the Danube River, where a part of Romania is today.

But Danny was excited to show me something that he considers especially noteworthy in a city full of special places. We walked toward the Porta Mesagne, through the pedestrian arch and across the narrow Via Appia going through Frederick II's enlarged arch. The Holy Roman emperor had built a bastion on the wall next to the gate to house soldiers who were resisting attackers. Much later, Charles V expanded this bastion, and this is pretty much what we see today. We went inside, where art exhibits and other displays are housed, and could see what the stone rooms were like.

We went outside through a door that opened through the

wall and into a section of what had been the *castellum aquae*, or once-closed cisterns that are now fully opened. These were vital, as the ancient city had a growing infrastructure and citizenry that needed water. The Romans certainly knew how to build cisterns as well as aqueducts to bring water long distances. But here, the water to fill this large network of cisterns was not too far away.

"The source of the water was Vito, which was about five and a half miles from Brindisi," Danny said. That place is on the provincial road to San Vito dei Normanni. "A millpond was made that consisted of collected water from four different springs." But the Romans, in this case, did not have to build one of their tall, sloping aqueducts to get that water into town. "From the millpond the water started down a specus [roofed channel] that got it to the city using only the force of gravity," Danny said. The slight difference in height from source to destination "permitted the path to be built underground with no need to be elevated with arches or bridges," he said.

The water entered the first tank, then fully enclosed, where its sediment and sand were filtered down naturally along the terra-cotta floor. It then flowed into the other tanks; there were perhaps three. From here, the water was piped throughout the ancient center.

Another interesting bit of history that Danny provided: The tanks were partially destroyed and covered by dirt in 1530 during the construction of a new city wall. Then, three hundred years later, the remnants of the cisterns were uncovered when the city built a new road (modern-day Via Cristoforo Colombo). Plans called for them to be destroyed to make way for a wider road, but scholars who love local history intervened, and the partial structures were saved. Much later, the tanks and bastion—the defensive building next to the large arch in Porta Mesagne—were part of a local pub, La Tortuga, until the 1980s. The pub was eventually closed.

We walked down the roadways that lead to the water's edge, following much of the original Via Appia to its end, and wandered past the church Saint Mary of the Angels, which sits at what was the intersection of Brundisium's two major roads. A few feet along the roadway is the Piazza Mercato. Danny said this was a Roman forum. "We know this because of the statues found here in the nineteen hundreds," Danny said. We go in for a closer look. A huge market fills the wide-open space. I look around and realize that it was here where, the night before, I had come in late at night for pizza, stumbling onto the place with no idea what it meant historically. Two or three restaurants use the space—vastly cleaned up after the daytime market ends—for outdoor dining.

Before we get to the water, near where I had spent time contemplating Caesar and Pompey the day before, Danny turns us left, a bit northward, through a variety of side streets. Within a few minutes, we stop for coffee and sit in a small square next to a modern, multistory structure housing a theater dedicated to the Italian composer Giuseppe Verdi.

Danny tells me the story. We are in a district known as Area archaeologica San Pietro degli Schiavoni. "Before the war, it was a typical neighborhood with small pitched-roof houses originally populated by the Slavs and the Albanians. The district was hit by bombs during World War Two. And so, it became a dilapidated and infamous neighborhood," he said.

"After the war [during the 1960s] they decided to raze it to initially build the courthouse, but during the excavations the remains of a medieval layer emerged. But at the time they didn't give much importance to medieval history, so most of them were destroyed.

"Continuing the excavations, Roman Brindisi emerged, the excavations stopped, and [the excavations] remained open for a long time. Many artifacts were dispersed and others stolen. It was then wisely decided to build the suspended theater, to preserve the area. Even in this case it took a long time."

The building in front of us, with the Roman ruins on the belowground floor surrounded by glass walls so passersby could look in, has the theater on a higher floor, along with offices above that. The ruins are a collection of beautifully preserved ancient rooms, Roman baths, and passageways, all contained within a well-lighted, calm, quiet space, immune from city clatter and covering perhaps fifty thousand square feet. We spent perhaps an hour inside walking on a steel walkway around the ruins, with Danny pointing out each element and explaining its function in vivid detail. I have wandered through many dusty ancient sites around Italy and elsewhere in the Mediterranean. This was the most enlightening visit of them all.

We walked outside. A few dozen feet away in a small open space stood a partial arch that once could have been a part of some ordinary medieval structure or part of the medieval church San Pietro degli Schiavoni, which welcomed Slavic and Albanian immigrants beginning in the fifteenth century. Brindisi, over the centuries, has been considered a major melting pot, drawing people from cultures all around the Mediterranean world. This slightly broken arch—carefully preserved and with a warm setting created around it—is a tribute to Brindisi's openness to various peoples and their cultures over the centuries.

We moved on, toward the nearby archaeological museum.

Danny gave a quick tour inside, knowing I had visited the place the day before. I was able to reexamine the bronzes on the top floor with Danny's explanation about where they were found and how they were recovered and restored. Then, outside and walking along the edge of the museum, the view of Brindisi's harbor and the sea beyond opened in front of us. We were on a high bluff paved with beautifully manicured stone. Next to us, high atop a long decline of steps to the water below—steps that reminded me of the Spanish Steps in Rome, albeit a smaller version—stood the Roman Columns of Brindisi. The one on the left, facing the sea, was intact; the other, next to it, was short and incomplete, having collapsed in a 1528 siege by an invading army.

I had always believed that the columns marked the end of the Via Appia. In reality, no one really knows what they represented. The website Atlas Obscura reports on the speculation that it marked the road's end, but it also suggests that they "could have been a point of reference for the sailors entering the port."

Whatever the reason, Danny absolutely dismisses what nearly all guidebooks say about it marking the end of the Appian Way. He believes, based on the materials used in the columns and other archaeological evidence, that Byzantines placed them there in the tenth century. He pointed out that the road would have ended at the water's edge, not on a high bluff with a long, steep slide downhill. It is more logical, he said, that it ended near the water, perhaps with an arch, at the edge of today's Piazza Vittorio Emanuele II, roughly six hundred feet away from the bottom of the columns' steps.

We were done for the day, but Danny had a couple of surprises left. He pointed to a building with a sign proclaiming it as the house of Virgil, the Roman historian who had joined

Horace and his party of diplomats on a mission to heal the strife between Octavian and Mark Antony. While there are those who believe it really is not his house, others believe it was where he died in 19 B.C.

Ancient writers tell us that Virgil had been meeting with Emperor Augustus in Athens. When done, he traveled to Megara in Western Greece, took sick, and decided to sail to Italy to recover. At some point, knowing he might die, this was when he asked friends to destroy his nearly complete manuscript of the *Aeneid* because he thought it was inferior. Thankfully, they did not follow his wishes. One source says he died aboard the ship in Brundisium's harbor. As usual, the fog of time clouds reality. Finding his house here reminded me of the sign marking Horace's house in Venosa, a made-up fantasy to draw tourists. Virgil's place could be legitimate, but, then again, maybe not.

Danny's second surprise was an offer to take me, the next day, on a car trip where we would make a sweep around the countryside north and west of Brindisi. He had insider's knowledge about two sections of the two roads—the Via Appia and the Via Traiana—that no travelers had ever seen and that appeared nowhere in any guidebook. In fact, archaeologists had just uncovered, less than two months before my visit, a section of the Via Appia.

The drive started early the next morning, heading north along a road that followed parts of the Via Traiana. Eventually, several miles into the countryside past beautiful olive groves, well manicured and perfectly spaced, and vineyards recently freed from their low-hanging fruit, Danny took a quick exit onto a narrow country road that likely sees more farm machinery than automobiles. He turned back south and then shifted onto an even narrower farm road. This was in the midst of fields, mostly fallow, but a few dozen feet ahead and to the side was an elongated mound of brush-covered soil.

Here and there, stone blocks and some brick peeked out of the clumped soil. These, Danny told me, were the sole remains of a Roman bridge that once soared over a wide river. The Via Traiana rose over it and carried armies, religious pilgrims, and merchants hauling goods north and south across its stony surface. Now, the only recognizable piece of what must have been a beautiful bridge is essentially an elongated section of a supporting arch. There must have been many arches for this bridge because a few hundred feet away was the natural spot where the bridge would have come down on the other side of this now nearly nonexistent river. All those stones and bricks disappeared over the centuries, ending up as walls around fields and in country homes and churches.

Danny knows that was the south end of the bridge because there is a small twentieth-century structure sitting on the bridge's Roman footings. The farmer, he said, built a "house" on it without any concern that he was abusing a piece of archaeological history. "Archaeologists know this is here; no one else does. But they do not do anything to protect it," he said. Then, turning to me, he added, "You come a long way from the United States to see the Via Appia and the Via Traiana because you care. Here they don't care."

He is frustrated. He has requested that the archaeological superintendency take steps to protect these and a handful of other sites he knows about. But he gets nowhere. This is a land of exceptional archaeological wonders, so many that there is rarely enough time, money, or people to investigate and preserve. The farmer only wants to farm. It is a wonder, Danny said, that the remains of this arch have not been bulldozed to level the land for another small section for growing crops.

We stood on top of the remains looking across a wide depression that had once held a mighty river on its way to help feed the Adriatic. "The river's modern name is Giancola," Danny said. "In Roman times, boats came inland from the Adriatic with food and pottery." There was a docking area upstream where boats would tie up and sell at a market. This is hard to imagine today looking at a wide swath that once held a river and now has the stubbly remains of a season's harvest.

As I looked toward the farmer's house sitting on those ancient, well-placed Roman stones, I could see a narrow ditch running east through the bottom of the depression. The river has shrunk over the centuries, and now the edge of this once wide and mighty course is used to move water for irrigating crops.

We headed back toward Brindisi, along the coastal road close to the water. We passed the remains of a tower near the point where the Giancola would have entered the sea. "This was built by Carlo V to watch out for the pirates that often came along the coast," Danny said. "They would often stop to get fresh water [from the river's mouth] for drinking." His reference to "Carlo" was the well-traveled Charles V, the Holy Roman emperor who reigned from 1519 to 1556. He made seven trips to Italy, spending a total of one thousand days in and around the country. The tower was a gift to help alert locals to pirate attacks.

As we neared Brindisi, Danny turned off and headed for the town of Mesagne, a few miles southeast of the port city, and from there we moved toward nearby Latiano, stopping on a lonely provincial road a mile or so before the village. He had something to show me, something exciting, he said.

We were going to an archaeological site known as Muro Tenente where, on August 5, 2021, just two months before my visit, archaeologists had uncovered a short section of the original Via Appia. They suspected it ran through the ancient village and was hidden for centuries under a small dirt road.

There is speculation that the village was known in ancient Roman times as Scamnum. But that village may have been located elsewhere. Archaeologists are not sure. So now it is simply Muro Tenente.

We parked just off the provincial road and walked through a grove of trees to the gate, left open for us by one of Danny's archaeologist friends, Christian Napolitano. The location of this gate and remains of pre-Roman walls built by the first occupiers, a people known as the Messapians, were only uncovered in 2016. A new gate has been installed and the crumbling walls, which in their glory circled the village, were restored just along the western portion of the ancient village grounds. The Romans came here and, in their usual fashion, took over the entire Salento peninsula, which we commonly refer to as Italy's heel, in 266 B.C. The Via Appia was built through here fewer than one hundred years later, arriving in Brundisium, just fifteen and a half miles away, in 191 B.C. Whatever its name, it was the last way station, or *statio*, along the Appian Way before Brundisium.

When the archaeologists discovered this patch of ground in 2016 with an ancient village buried beneath a field twenty acres in size, they found many tombs dating between the sixth and fourth centuries B.C. with Messapic inscriptions. The newly found section of the Via Appia was a short stretch, perhaps 150 feet long and just inside the west gate. It is in line with the modern SS7/Via Appia Nuova, a short distance away. Danny pointed out that the surface stone, loose and crumbled, was not of the quality of other sections of the road farther north and west. "This area was too far from the quality stone used in other sections, so they had to use local materials. The stones were smaller and cobble-like, not like the big stones in Rome," he said.

The next day, Danny said we would take another ride north—his partner, Antonella Romano, would join us—past the site of the crumbling Roman arch on the ancient Via Traiana bridge to an archaeological site run known as Scavi D'Egnazia, or Excavations of Egnatia. Horace, in his satire about the journey, referred to the village, in still another spelling, as Gnatia. He mocked what he and his party witnessed while staying there. Erik Jensen describes it thusly:

> As before at Fundi, the company was amused by the pretensions of the locals, although this time the claim is a religious rather than a political one. The parallel might suggest that here again the company received local official hospitality, but we cannot be certain of it.

Egnazia, whose name is like the ancient road across the Balkans, is located along the coastal road SP90 and nearly thirty-six miles north of Brindisi. The ruins are august. They cover approximately one hundred acres and, in addition to the ruins of the ancient town, there is a necropolis, or cemetery. Also impressive is the museum. That was our first stop. A host greeted us there, and Danny told him we wanted to visit the ruins and walk along the Via Traiana. The man shook his head. "It is closed." Danny, a professional tour guide who knows the wiles and ways of getting around things in Italy, pulled the man aside and spoke quietly, like he was the man's best friend.

Moments later, Danny told Antonella and me that the man promised to look the other way if we quietly left the museum, walked several hundred feet to the ruins entrance, stepped over the low gate and entered the site. We did as instructed. Danny had promised we would not walk through the ruins themselves but look, from a strategically placed platform, across the sea of excavated rooms, bathhouses, and in the distance, a forum area.

Through the middle of all this ran a wide Roman road that was the Via Traiana. This, of course, was built to high Roman standards more than a century after Horace's journey. But it likely encompassed an earlier road through the center of the town and would have been the route of the party. It was here that Horace was reminded that "the gods live a carefree life." And there his satire ends suddenly with, "[Brundisium's] the end of a long road and this story."

We paced a bit around the platform, which surrounded some pieces of ruins, took photographs, and lamented that we could not wander into the stony maze. The walk back to the museum that thankfully was open was invigorating and the displays beautifully done. I spent some time admiring a statue of the Greek goddess of agriculture and mother of Persephone, Demeter—like Diana, one of my favorite goddesses. We drove back to Brindisi. I was satiated with what Danny had shown me over three days.

I spent time following that visit learning that an earlier village, probably buried beneath Gnatia's ancient ruins we saw that day, began as a Bronze Age settlement in the fifteenth century B.C. Around the eighth century B.C., the Messapic people ruled here and along the entire heel of Italy. The Romans came

The beginning of the preserved section of the Via Appia, Rome, in the Parco Regionale dell'Appia Antica.

A street along the side of what once was the Roman forum in Ariccia's hilltop that leads to the route of the ancient Via Appia below.

Remains of columns at the Temple of Diana down the mountain village of Nemi, a short distance from the route of the Via Appia.

Part of the Temple of Diana, seen downhill from Nemi. The temple is closed to visitors and the structure under construction will house an archaeological center when the grounds reopen.

The remains of an ancient structure named for two Roman emperors, at the ancient village of Forum Appi, now covered over by the modern village of Borgo Faiti. The canal, known as the Decennovian and now much narrower, was where the poet Horace and his fellow travelers left their walk along the Via Appia and boarded a mule-drawn barge to Terracina.

A short section of the ancient Via Appia, almost hidden away behind a fence and stone wall in Terracina's Old Town, that sits, well preserved, on private property.

A more public section of the ancient road, with most original stones intact, runs through what once was the Roman forum in Terracina and now is a wide-open town square.

One of the best-preserved sections of the ancient Via Appia outside of villages and archaeological sites is found north and south of the tiny town of Itri. This section has had many of its original stones removed and reused in old buildings.

The Tomb of Cicero, at Formia, near where the Roman philosopher, writer, government official, and lawyer had one of his homes, sits at the edge of the ancient road, now paved over for modern vehicles. His body is generally believed not to be here. The tomb was built sometime during the second half of the first century A.D., a century after his death.

The original Via Appia making a short run through the archaeological ruins of Minturnae, near modern Minturno.

The remains of the coliseum of ancient Capua, amid the ruins of the gladiator training school made famous by Spartacus, the slave who led his fellow slaves in revolt against Rome. Rebel survivors were crucified along the Via Appia from Rome to Capua. The town is now known as Santa Maria Capua Vitere (Santa Maria of Old Capua).

(Above) The Ponte Leproso Bridge, over the Sabato River on the outskirts of Benevento, was built during the Roman era and is one of a handful of such bridges still being used throughout Italy. This one is for walking and riding bicycles— no motorized vehicles allowed.

This road, paved and primarily used for farm vehicles, follows the ancient Via Appia route through the countryside outside of Benevento.

Emperor Trajan ordered a coastal route as a break off from the original, more inland Via Appia route, both ending at Brindisi. The new section became the Via Traiana. The Arch of Trajan sits at the point where the new route headed southeast toward the Adriatic coastline.

The Roman poet Horace and fellow travelers, as well as the writer Virgil, after reaching Brindisi, journeyed the short distance from Brindisi to Taranto. Horace later wrote about visiting the river Galaesus there, today's Galeso. He longingly described it as beautiful but now it flows through a badly overgrown industrial area; the modern Via Appia is nearby.

(Above) Roman ruins were uncovered when a modern building was going to be constructed in Brindisi. The building's design was changed, and the multi-story structure was built to allow this ground-level display.

Part of an ancient figure discovered along the shallow edge of the Adriatic Sea. Now on display in Brindisi's archaeological museum.

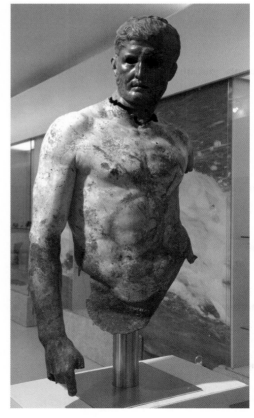

(Above) A short section of the Via Appia in an area between Taranto and Brindisi. The section was uncovered in August 2021, a little more than a month before the author's visit. This site has the modern name of Muro Tenente.

On the edge of a farmer's field, just off the Adriatic coast, sits a large mound of earth covering the remains of one end of a Roman bridge that was part of the Via Traiana. Stone pillars and a low wall, examined by archaeological guide and friend Danny Vitale, peek out of the vegetation-covered mound.

(Above) The Via Traiana pushes its way through the ruins of Roman Egnathia, perched on the Adriatic coast north of Brindisi. The poet Horace and his fellow travelers spent a night in Egnathia more than a century before the Traiana was built.

A Roman milestone, or *miliario*, for the Via Traiana sits along a modern road sweeping around a marina in the city of Bari. It was placed here in the 1930s by officials in dictator Mussolini's government and may, or may not, denote its original position on the ancient road.

The route of the Via Traiana flows through the village of Troia, a few feet below the modern Via Regina Margherita.

The remains of a short section of the Via Traiana have been uncovered in a small archaeological site of the Roman town of Herdonia. The town was much larger in Roman times but was lost to modern eyes after it was destroyed by the Carthaginian general Hannibal during the Second Punic War.

(Above) These stones are believed by many to be part of the ancient Via Egnatia, which ran across the Balkans, from the western Adriatic coast to Byzantium, now known as Istanbul. This spot is in the hills above the North Macedonian village of Radožda, located on Lake Ohrid.

A lone, headless statue with no name, missing a friend that once was on a pedestal beside her, sits in the midst of the Roman ruins of Heraclea Lyncestis on the edge of the North Macedonian city of Bitola. The Via Traiana, now buried, ran through these ruins, and continued into northern Greece.

(Above) The ancient city of Philippi in northern Greece, where Octavian, the future Augustus, and Mark Antony defeated Caesar's murderers, Brutus and Cassius. A century later, St. Paul preached to the Philippians and made his first converts on European soil.

A newly restored section of the Via Egnatia leading to the Plain of Philippi, now a collection of farmers' fields. Alongside it is Soula Tsolaki, a guide and the author's friend, based in nearby Kavala, once the ancient city of Neapolis.

The end of the Via Egnatia, at the Milion (cq) Stone now under restoration in the center of Istanbul. This is the remaining piece of four columns holding up arches that marked this place—the beginning and end of all roads leading to and leaving Constantinople, once Byzantium and now Istanbul.

The interior of the vast Roman-built *Piscina Mirabilis*, or "wondrous pool", was not for swimming but for the storage of water for the many Roman palaces or palazzi where affluent Romans, including the dictator Julius Caesar and a handful of emperors, had summer homes. This pool is in Bacoli, ancient Bauli, on the Campanian coast.

in the third century B.C. With the Gnatians came the cult of the sun and fire. Pliny wrote that "there is a sacred stone, upon which, when wood is placed, flame immediately bursts forth." And it was likely this cult and their religious ceremonies that our poet Horace ridiculed in the closing lines of his satire.

The town was dying out by the sixth century A.D., but the moment of its last gasp was not known. Over time, much of its walls that once surrounded the city were appropriated for building projects, a typical Italian practice in the days before archaeological standards were established. And even then, much of the material that made up the ancient cities, including in this place, were carted away under the dark of night.

Later, Danny took me to visit a friend, Marco Cazzato, the proprietor of a small B&B, Regina Viarum Casavacanza. He had refurbished a nineteenth-century building for the venture, and, during construction, workers broke through the floor. Beneath were the unmistakable stones of a Roman street. It was not the Via Appia seeing the light of day. The path of that roadway was a few dozen feet away from Marco's building under a paved-over city street. Construction immediately stopped and archaeologists were called in. They documented the area and eventually allowed work to proceed, but Marco decided to find a way to display it for his guests. He opened the floor and put a few feet of the street under glass, glass sturdy enough to walk on, so visitors can see the ancient stones below. A nice touch.

My time in Brindisi was nearing an end. But before I would head up the southeastern Italian coast, following the Via Traiana route to Bari, ancient Barium, and then westward, to Benevento and eventually Rome, I needed to leave Italy and go east, across the Adriatic, and find another Roman road, the Via Egnatia. The plan was to follow it from Albania and across the southwest corner of North Macedonia, Northern Greece, and into Turkey. A gentleman named Gnaeus Egnatius, proconsul of Roman Macedonia, ordered it built to high Roman standards in the second century B.C. This, too, was a major accomplishment in the days of the republic's expansion eastward. It spread across the Balkans all the way to what was then Byzantium, later known as Constantinople, and today's Istanbul.

The Via Appia, the Via Traiana, and the Via Egnatia tied Rome militarily, commercially, and, in the Later Roman Empire, religiously to the beautiful city on the Bosphorus.

10

A MACEDONIAN LAKE

Such was the Via Egnatia, 540 miles long, which
connected the Adriatic Sea to the Black Sea. It was on this
road that, in 48 B.C., a Roman knight, Vibullius Rufus,
travelled "night and day, changing horses at every town
to gain speed," to warn Pompey of Caesar's approach.
—American explorer Victor W. von Hagen

It was time to jump across the Adriatic and join the Via Egnatia, a road almost as old as the Via Appia and just as important to the republic and later the empire. By following this ancient road—on foot along a few very short historic stretches and driving along its length on modern parallel roads—I would go all the way to Istanbul where it ended. Its stopping point is just a few dozen feet short of the Hagia Sophia, first a Christian church, then a mosque, then secularized and turned into a museum, and finally, in July 2020, back to a mosque.

The Via Egnatia, started in 146 B.C. and completed in 120 B.C., was the first Roman road constructed outside of Italy. As an extension of the Via Appia, it originally was a military road that, with its Italian predecessor, eventually connected Rome with what was then known as Byzantium, which had consistently been pro-Roman while still independent of that great Western power. Some writers refer to it by its Greek name, Byzantion, but its name derives from its founder, a gentleman named Byzas, who, according to Greek legend, built the town around 657 B.C.

Emperor Constantine, in A.D. 324, named this magnificent Greek city on the European side of the Bosphorus New Rome and in 330, seven years before his death, it was renamed Constantinople in his honor. That name held until the early twentieth century when it became Istanbul.

The Via Egnatia—envisioned by Gnaeus Egnatius, one of the earliest governors of Roman Macedonia—began in two places on the Adriatic coast: Apollonia and Dyrrachium in Illyricum (modern Albania) and crossed, west to east, three ancient lands. At that time, Macedonia was the large geographic area beyond Illyricum. The land between the eastern edge of Macedonia and the Black Sea was known as Thrace. The name Macedonia still perseveres today, divided between the new nation of North Macedonia and Northern Greece, which holds on to the name as a province.

After leaving Illyria, the Egnatia crossed the southwest corner of what is now North Macedonia before tumbling down into Northern Greece and then eastward to Byzantium, giving Rome access to the Aegean, eastern Mediterranean, the Black Sea, and Asia. The historian Bettany Hughes, author of *Istanbul: A Tale of Three Cities,* says it succinctly: "The Via Egnatia irrevocably turned [Byzantium] from a staging post into a destination." She also tells us that it followed the route of an earlier road in Illyria called the Road to Candavia, adding, "Philip and Alexander's palace at Pella in Macedonia was built beside the forerunner of the Egnatian Way." This route was flanked by temples and burials, and "Alexander the Great would have marched out past these temples of the dead on his mission to conquer the world."

Roughly three centuries after Alexander, the Via Egnatia was used to move armies of Roman generals such as Pompey, Caesar, Mark Antony, Caesar's murderers (Brutus and Cassius), and many emperors, playing a role in civil wars and the subjugation of Eastern peoples. Emperor Trajan, a roadbuilder of immense reputation in Italy proper, undertook extensive repairs to the road prior to his campaign of A.D. 113 against the Parthians, located in Iran's northeast. While surviving milestones honor his roadbuilding prowess, they conveniently do not mention his lack of success in Parthia. He died, frustrated, in A.D. 117.

A handful of other emperors also ordered the road maintained, including Hadrian, Marcus Aurelius, Septimius Severus, and Caracalla. Even co-emperors Diocletian and Maximian, in the late third century, contributed to maintaining the road with significant repairs. Such repairs and which emperor ordered them were usually marked on *miliaria*, or mileposts placed a Roman mile (1,620 yards) apart. One source says there must have been five hundred of them along the Via Egnatia; today, only thirty-eight have been recovered. I saw only three of them on my journey. And they were not in the places the Romans first set them. They are only set for display in museums or a village square.

And the road, thanks to all these restoration efforts, survived for centuries as a major commercial route, especially in winter when the Adriatic, Aegean, and Ionian Seas were too rough for ships. They became pilgrimage routes from west to east during the Christian period. The apostle Paul followed significant portions of the road on his journey from Neapolis (modern Kavala, Greece) to Philippi, a handful of miles away, and Thessaloniki, preaching to Jews and gentiles alike.

After the Romans, the road through the Eastern Roman Empire was important to what became the Byzantine Empire and later the Ottoman Empire. During the Christian period, the European armies of the First Crusade, beginning in 1096, used the road to get to Constantinople, where they would prepare, under the watchful eye of the Byzantine government that long before had succeeded the Romans, for their forays into the Middle East toward Muslim-held Jerusalem.

I had to sort out that logistical issue preventing me from driving my French rental car into Albania or Turkey. Only North Macedonia and Greece were acceptable. The Turkey problem was easily solvable. I had a friend there, Lütfi Baydar, who had agreed to arrange a contract driver to take me over the border between Greece and Turkey, and Lütfi would meet me on the other side.

He said I could safely park my rental at the border. Once over, we would drive the three hours to Istanbul and spend a couple of days exploring the Via Egnatia's historic relationship there. I knew Lütfi was a historian at heart and that he knew well his country's ancient past. Then, he would drive me back to the border, where the special driver would return me to Kipoi where I could recover my French car. Then I could slowly make my way back to Brindisi.

Albania would be trickier. My only solution was to leave my car in Brindisi, take a ferry to the port at Durrës, and rent a local car for the three days I wanted to spend there. My Brindisi friend, Danny, offered a solution. He was curious about my project and wanted to see the Albanian Via Egnatia portions for himself. He suggested going with me on the ferry, taking his Italian car, and we would spend those few days exploring the ancient road between Durrës and Apollonia and the North Macedonia border.

If everything fell into place, that would be an excellent solution. Unfortunately, Covid pandemic problems unique to Albania got in the way. That trip had to be canceled.

Everything else happened perfectly as planned. My first four-week-long, cross-Adriatic journey would begin between Brindisi and the Greek port of Igoumenitsa, far to the south of where the Via Egnatia route would leave Albania. I would be able to travel through that corner of North Macedonia, then back down into Northern Greece to begin the journey across the northern Greek province of Macedonia. I would then cross the border into Turkey and catch my ride to Istanbul. All I had to do was drive from Igoumenitsa and into North Macedonia far to the north for my first Balkan stay on Lake Ohrid in the village of the same name. There, I hoped to encounter preserved pieces of that ancient Roman road.

The ferry ride lasted a day. During lunch, I fell in with a group of Eastern European truck drivers who offered a seat at their table. The room was crowded and noisy. I sat down, and the men—their cargoes safely stowed in their semitrailers and parked in the bowels of the big oceangoing ferry—were full of questions. Why was I going to Greece? I told them about the Via Egnatia. They knew it, having driven along the modern parallel route many times. They shuddered when I told them I would cross the border into Turkey.

"Oh, that is a long wait for us," one of them said. "Customs, you know. It is a nightmare, and it can take hours." But they said if I am merely in a car, it should be quick. I certainly hoped he was correct. My Turkish friend, Lütfi, had assured me that everything was taken care of. The contract driver would have the necessary paperwork, and the crossing would be smooth.

In the early evening, we landed at the Greek port city of Igoumenitsa, just a short distance to the east of the island of Corfu, which had disappeared as darkness descended while we were arriving in port. I drove to my nearby lodgings for the night, planning an early morning trip north to a halfway stop in Kozani, Greece.

Igoumenitsa is a comfortable town with a lively center and a modern, walkable outdoor mall full of restaurants, bars, and young people having a good time. I checked in, dropped off luggage, found a place to eat my first fully Greek dinner, and turned in. I was tired. There is not much to do on a six-to-eight-hour ferry ride and not many comfortable spots to relax in, so I wanted to be ready for my long drive in the morning. My return trip, a month away, would be overnight on the ferry heading back to Brindisi, and I vowed to get a sleeping compartment. I had learned long ago the wisdom of such a nighttime arrangement.

Morning dawned. I headed out of this pleasant city and followed my car's navigator toward my destination of Kozani. This was about halfway to my ultimate destination of Ohrid, North Macedonia. After a few miles north on a nicely built interstate-quality highway, I started noticing a strange series of signs telling me that I was traveling on the Egnatia Odos. This caught me by surprise. Here I was driving through the Greek province of Epirus, miles away from the ancient route much farther to the north in the Greek province of Macedonia.

That evening, in my lodgings in Kozani, a small town in the western part of that province, I got on the internet and searched for Egnatia Odos. I discovered that *odos* can be translated as street, road, or way. Its Italian counterpart, of course, is *via*. It was a massive construction project, beginning in 1994 and completed fifteen years later. Interestingly, the formal numerical highway designation is E90, and this designation is used for a European highway that crosses several countries. Greece chose to name its section, running 416 miles from Igoumenitsa to the Turkish border, in honor of the ancient road and its great importance from classical through medieval times. From Kozani, it meets the ancient route near Edessa, running parallel to it all the way to the Turkish border.

In Central Greece, the modern route plows through the Pindus Mountains. I knew the name Pindus. That was the general area where Caesar defeated Pompey at the Battle of Pharsalus. This range, often referred to as the spine of Greece, runs south-southeast from Albania and across the central mainland.

I had to keep in mind that the relatively new nation of North Macedonia, my destination for the next day, was indeed the northern part of the larger ancient province. The two similar names for the Greek province and the new nation to the north can be very confusing.

But I had to leave the Egnatia Odos at Kozani. There, the European roadway swung northeast toward Thessaloniki. To get to North Macedonia I exited onto E65 and headed due north. The drive through this part of central mainland Greece is a wonderful visual experience. The mountains, once seen by Caesar's and Pompey's armies, are covered with a variety of pines, and in the valleys I was driving through juniper forests. Occasionally, I would deliberately leave the highway and go onto secondary roads and into small pastoral villages past flocks of sheep being moved down from the high pastures to winter quarters below and farmers on tractors tilling their fields. These roads often took me higher up on mountainous slopes and offered magnificent views.

Crossing the border from Greece into North Macedonia was a smooth process. My documents were accepted, I passed the quick Covid test, and I was sent on my way with a happy wave by the young, masked woman brandishing a long cotton swab. They had my contact information, so I assumed if the test was positive, I would hear from them.

Leaving the border station, the road into North Macedonia was rough and not well maintained. A scattering of abandoned, communist-era buildings did not offer a pleasant visual intro-duction to the new nation, which had gained independence as a successor state of the former Yugoslavia in 1991. Then, it was known simply as Macedonia. But that rubbed the Greeks across the southern border wrong; their adjoining Greek prov-ince also is called Macedonia. Eventually, a compromise was reached, and the Slavic nation added "North" to its name in 2019, just two years before my visit. The Greeks still grumble about this I am told, and a couple of North Macedonians with whom I spoke are not happy either. It was a geopolitical night-mare with no solution pleasing to either side.

With that pretrip research bouncing around in my head, the landscape a few miles beyond the border crossing gradu-ally opened. The road, a narrow two-lane affair, became better maintained. It was taking me through stunning country, its low rolling hills jammed with deciduous trees so thick the hills look impenetrable. It was early October, and the fall colors were equal to those I have seen in New England.

The main crop here seems to be apples, especially around the town of Resen, another small place in this lush countryside that was well-known in Roman times. Wooden stands selling different varieties are everywhere, one after another. I stop at one. Baskets filled with seven or eight different kinds are spread out along the road's edge. A woman greets me. I indicate I want the best eating type, and she points to two baskets, urging me to select what I want. I take just two. I leave and a mile or so down the road pull over. I wash one apple off with water from my bottle, contemplate its bright redness with tiny hints of yellow, and take a bite. It is almost as if the crack that the sound of my bite made could be heard bouncing off the hillside like a gunshot. My god. I am in heaven.

As a youth in Idaho, my mother would take me to apple orchards, where she would get different varieties for baking or eating. A farmer once handed me an apple freshly picked from a tree. I bit into it. It was the first time I heard that crack, and my mouth filled with an indescribable sweetness. For years, well into advanced adulthood, I searched for that apple of my youth, never finding it. Here, in North Macedonia, I found it. I stopped at another stand and selected a bag full of the same variety. Eating apples became my passion for the next five days.

Between the border and Lake Ohrid, it seemed that every house along the roadway featured piles of firewood. The whine of power saws chased me down the highway as everyone seemed to be getting ready for winter in an economy that depends mostly on wood heating. The forests, full of those deciduous trees soon to lose their colorful leaves as winter sets in, provide plenty of wood. The smell of freshly sawn logs hung in the air, wafting through my open window. The taste of those apples and the smell of newly cut trees fueled this Idaho native's memories of home.

Lake Ohrid is considered one of Europe's—and the world's— deepest and oldest, its waters lapping against pleasing public areas of the village. Most lakes eventually fill with sediment and last only a hundred thousand years. This lake, with natural filtration through underground streams, could be three million years old.

The town of Ohrid was a Greek settlement with the original name of Lychnidos. Sources say the name Ohrid likely is a derivation of that ancient Greek name when it shifted into Albanian and Slavic languages. The village existed in the time of Alexander the Great's father, Philip II of Macedon, in the fourth century B.C. He predated the Romans' arrival in the area at the end of the third century and beginning of the second. They likely kept the Greek name. Records show that the name Ohrid for the village and the lake did not appear until the ninth century A.D.

The village sits high up on the eastern edge of Lake Ohrid. The important but smaller village of Struga is a few miles away at the lake's northern tip, and the road down the west side eventually would cross over low-lying hills into Albania. The route of the ancient Via Egnatia across Albania is believed to have entered North Macedonia near the middle of the lake's western edge and run along the shoreline past Struga, skirting the edge of Ohrid village. There, it turns eastward, away from the lake and along my apple highway, through Resen and toward the ancient city of Heraclea Lyncestis, now an archaeological site next to modern Bitola. From there, the Via Egnatia would continue southeasterly across the border and into the Greek province of Macedonia at Edessa.

I hope to travel the route, which I know to be the Egnatia under much of the modern pavement, around the lake's northern end as far as the very small hamlet of Radožda. If I go much farther, I will hit Albania. I am hopeful that there will be some indication during the drive that I will come across a short segment of the ancient road. A detailed, authoritative guidebook, *Via Egnatia on Foot: A Journey into History,* recognizes a short section in the hills above Radožda as a possible section but leaves it open to speculation.

At my lodgings, I asked my proprietor, Sonja, if she knew anyone who could offer a tour, someone who might have special knowledge of the Via Egnatia. Through her friend Marina Ilieva, I was referred to Valentina Godoroska. A few hours later I got the message: "A colleague of mine, [Valentina], will be available. She is an archeologist, too, and working on the project about 'guess what'—Via Egnatia! So, gladly I'm sending to you her number."

This opened the door to a remarkable day with a guide who really knows her subject. She is high on my list of important guides that shared their extensive knowledge with me on my journey, folks like Danny Vitale in Brindisi, Alexandros Lamprianidis at the ruins of Philippi, and Soula Tsolaki at Kavala, who took me on hidden stretches of the Via Egnatia that, despite my pretrip research, I had no idea existed. And this is what Valentina Godoroska was about to do.

Valentina told me to meet her the next day in Struga at a large coffee bar attached to a modern restaurant sitting on the lakeshore. She was on time. She talked about how studies of the Via Egnatia were gaining in popularity, and she was involved in trying to find the precise route into North Macedonia from Albania and determine where it rolled around the lake to Ohrid while heading to Resen. I realized through this coffee-driven conversation that I must always keep in mind that the Via Egnatia is without exception close by, if not actually underfoot.

She is mysterious when I ask her what awaited us, saying only, "You will see."

On the ride south down the lake's west side, she told me the road is heavily used in summer because of all the lakeside activities. This area, after all, is now geared toward tourism as the relatively new nation of North Macedonia is trying to expand its economy well beyond sheep and apples. It is a beautiful area and, while I am not a tourist on this trip, I can certainly see the possibilities: boat rides, fishing, camping. Ohrid, especially, hopes to draw a large summertime crowd.

In winter in ancient times, Valentina tells me, travelers on the road we are on, believed to be the route of the ancient Egnatia, would split off from the lakeside Egnatia and go around and above Struga. Then, it would rejoin the road to Ohrid where it swung around the northern edge of the mountain called Galičica, which from its summit to the lake is a national park, including all the lakeside villages south of Ohrid. After going around the mountain, the ancient route straightens out near Resen, the site of my apple paradise. This is a small village, just twenty-three miles to the southeast of Ohrid. In Roman times, builders pushed the Via Egnatia through its center and then beyond another twenty or so miles to connect with Heraclea Lyncestis and then on to Greek Macedonia.

It is a lovely early fall drive along the lake. Traffic is light, and as we approach the tiny hamlet of Radožda, she tells me to pull off. Again, the smell of freshly chopped wood dominates, and stacks of it are everywhere, scattered among the various houses and buildings.

"We are walking," she instructs. With our backs to the lake, we march uphill along a very narrow cobblestone street between two or three buildings, stroll past families cutting and stacking wood, and head up a moderately steep pathway just wide enough for a tractor, perhaps, or a cart pulled by a donkey or a mule. The cobblestones end, and the hard-packed dirt pathway, six or seven feet wide, is a bit wet but walkable. After several hundred feet of walking, we round a curve and there, just ahead, are gleaming white stones embedded deep in the pathway.

The presence of these stones, the pieces of curbs that remain along the sides, prove in Valentina's mind and in the minds of several of her colleagues that this was the Via Egnatia, a road more than two thousand years old that now is used to haul logs. The stony section, which we walked the length of, is only five hundred meters long, Valentina tells me, or about sixteen hundred feet.

"The villagers use this dirt road to bring logs down from the mountains," Valentina says. "In the olden days, this was fine, because that's what it was built for. Modern vehicles are destroying parts of it."

She told me that a mentor of hers, Ohrid archaeologist Pasko Kuzman, discovered this segment several decades ago. Excited about his discovery, he reportedly told colleagues, "I kissed the stones of the Via Egnatia when I found it!" The guidebook notes Kuzman's role but says that "new evidence" suggests the road could have been a bit higher over the mountain. But Valentina stands by her mentor's pronouncement.

I am in Ohrid for four days and have plenty of time to explore this part of ancient Macedonia. First, I need to check out a report that the town, today with roughly forty thousand residents, at the beginning of the Common Era had 365 churches and was called the Jerusalem of the Balkans. I asked my friend Marina about this.

"The story of Jerusalem of the Balkans is from the seventeenth century when Turkish writer Evliya Çelebi visited

Macedonia and counted [that many] churches, one for each day of the year," she told me. I asked how many were left in this small town. "Around seventy of them are still in use, but the rest are under the ground and waiting to be discovered."

Çelebi was a traveler, not so ancient, along the Via Egnatia in the sixteen hundreds. He has been described as "one of the most celebrated Ottoman travelers, who journeyed for more than forty years throughout the territories of the Ottoman Empire and adjacent lands." The entry, from *Britannica,* goes on to point out that "Evliya possessed a vivid imagination, occasionally mixing fact and fantasy; he described places he could not possibly have visited. [He is] noted for his fascinating anecdotes and charming style." So, could the number of churches be a bit exaggerated? Marina accepts it as fact, and she knows her town very well. I will trust her word.

My B&B sits, as do many of the more recently built houses of the town, on a hill that follows the curve of the lake's shoreline. Near my building, along a short, narrow street, is a restored Roman theater dating back to antiquity. It has the traditional stony circular seating area, or cavea, and a scaena, or stage. The view of the lake and the mountains from above the stage must have been as pleasurable to see as what was happening with players and musicians below. This must be a perfect modern venue for summertime plays and musical events.

A small terrace off my room offers a sweeping view of the town that is a short walk downhill, a walk that I took often. It is along a series of narrow streets and walkways with long stone steps toward the modern lakeside town, and I passed craft shops, including one turning out hand-carved wooden figures that follow the culture of this part of Macedonia. I purchased a few examples of the work by a young man toiling in his small shop, Woodcarving Gallery Tron. Dragan Nelovski said he was following in the tradition of his father and his grandfather in this shop. His family's work is on display, ranging from carved religious icons to mythical creatures, gods, and goddesses.

Nearby, I found a tiny shop selling silver jewelry. The craftsman, who did not offer his name, sold me a piece of handmade, finely detailed earrings. I am not usually one to take home gifts from a working trip, but I could not resist. I wanted to have a few objects by which to remember Ohrid. It is a truly wonderful place surrounding a large inlet of the lake, deep and mysterious.

The people I met over four days spoke some English but mostly the Macedonian language, a south Slavic tongue that has traces of Bulgarian. Special government documents for the minority population say those peoples can speak their own languages. For these folks, Macedonian is a second language. This is a place where a visitor can hear Greek, Albanian, Turkish, Romani, Serbian, Bosnian, and Aromanian. Albanian is considered a "co-official" language along with Macedonian. It can be quite confusing, a man behind the counter in a cigar shop said. But such rules and regulations reflect, I suspect, a brand-new nation of mixed cultures trying to sort itself out.

North Macedonia was politically carved out of other nations, much like Yugoslavia was created after World War I, so different cultures were mixed with one another. Most of the people I talked to, including a Greek friend in central mainland Greece, express frustration with the political manipulations that tossed these disparate "Balkanians" together. I cannot imagine how a people who grew up under communism, then had their piece of Yugoslavia set free in 1991, followed by having a new name thrust on them in 2019, can possibly feel. I do know that whatever their culture, they are among the most friendly and helpful folks I met on this extended trip that covered four nations. I want to return so I have time to ride a boat on Lake Ohrid and once again wander the shops, eat excellent regional food, and relax on a small terrace overlooking an ancient Roman theater and the lakeside below.

I head on the modern road, the E65, that follows the Via Egnatia route from Ohrid around the base of Galičica and through apple country and the village of Resen to Bitola, about fifty miles from that clear blue lake. Bitola is not stunning, but it has a transformed city center drawn out of medieval structures. My rooms, very modern, warm, and pleasant, are in an older building, perhaps prewar, just a few blocks from this center filled with shops of all kinds, plus restaurants, and bars.

On my walk to breakfast each morning, I cross the grounds of a home for retired military officers. To my right is the main street. To my left is the museum that once was a military school. Interestingly, this school, at the turn of the twentieth century, was attended by Mustafa Kemal, who later became a military general, political leader, and reformer, as well as the founder of the modern Turkish republic. He served as president from 1923 until his death in 1938. The honorific title "Atatürk" was added to his name.

I was struck by the fact that he was born in Thessaloniki in Greece, educated here in this northern part of Macedonia, and then ended up creating the Turkish nation farther to the east. Of course, from his birth to his early forties, the Balkans that included all these political pieces were part of the long-lived Ottoman Empire, which collapsed in 1922 in the aftermath of World War I. That empire had lasted nearly 470 years following the Muslim takeover of Constantinople from the Byzantine Empire in 1453. He essentially carved Turkey out of the dying Ottoman Empire. As one who likes to track the footsteps of the ancient generals, emperors, and statesmen, I wandered the halls of his former school, now a sufficient museum, to connect with someone a bit more modern. A satisfying visit indeed.

It is easy to understand that Bitola is part of the site of one of the oldest villages in Macedonia. In the fourth century B.C., Philip II of Macedon, Alexander the Great's father, ordered the building of Heraclea in the ancient region of Lyncestis. The Romans came in 148 B.C. Those ruins, just a mile or so from the museum's front door, host a scattering of Roman-era structures. I paid the fee, and the man who sold the ticket left his tiny office at the front gate, walked to another gate, unlocked it, and motioned me inside. I saw only two other patrons that day, a father and son. The father, who seemed to know his history, spoke authoritatively to his son, explaining each area in detail. The boy, about nine or ten, appeared captivated by it all and asked a lot of questions. A future historian or archaeologist.

They moved out of earshot. Then, the gate opened, and Viktor Bushinoski walked into the enclosure. He shook my hand and said he was a guide at the site and could he show me around? No charge, he said. "It's my job, and today it is my turn to be here." From Viktor, I learned that the ruins I was seeing represented only 15 percent of Heraclea's original layout. There are new areas being explored, east and southwest against the nearby hills. That could expand the site by several acres. He pointed out that the Via Egnatia entered this spot near—or perhaps even on—the road I entered on. Evidence of the ancient road was found beneath the house built next to the site's parking area. The original road would then be under a small modern tract running along the edge of the site.

We walked through many of the rooms, including areas seemingly blocked off from the public. "When I am with you, we can enter." Viktor smiled. Other rooms had stunning mosaics on the floors, exposed to wind, rain, and snow. Most of the mosaics were laid down at the end of the Roman Empire, between A.D. 490 and 550. Heraclea itself gradually slid into a state of decline and was abandoned by the Middle Ages. Bitola, now North Macedonia's second-largest city, grew close by as a town with churches, mosques, and consulates occupied by a handful of other nations.

We walked along the tops of partial walls enclosing several of those rooms, looking down upon the thousands of colored bits of stone that made magnificent scenes of flora and fauna. Then, in other rooms along the edge of the huge stone theater, which once had seating for as many as twenty-five hundred persons, the floors were covered in clean gravel. Mosaics were beneath. Viktor said that eventually all the mosaics I just saw would be covered in the same way. Archaeologists lay a heavy, perforated plastic sheet over the stones, and then cover that with clean gravel. This is necessary, of course, to preserve these wonderful pieces of ancient art. Permanent protective structures can be built when the necessary funds are found, and the mosaics can be unveiled. Until then, visitors will just view photographs that will eventually be placed around the site.

It was time to move on. The Greek border crossing is only nine or ten miles southeast of Bitola, and I would be following a modern road built over much of the ancient Egnatia all the way to Edessa, my first stop along the Greek portion of the route. This line of travel, across Northern Greece to the Turkish border, essentially keeps me in the southern half of what was ancient Macedonia and is now Greece's province of Macedonia. I still had adventures before me, good guides to meet, and sites such as Pella, where Philip II ruled and Alexander was born, and Philippi, where Mark Antony and Octavian destroyed Brutus and Cassius. The armies of the good guys and the bad marched along the Via Egnatia, as did the apostle Paul and his companion Saint Silas. If I'm lucky, I'll find their footsteps to follow as well.

11

TO PELLA

Thessalonica, the most important city in all the Balkans, and the Aegean even before Byzantium became the imperial capital, has always rivaled Constantinople, and sometimes served as an alternate capital.

—Writer Firmin O'Sullivan

Returning to Greece, across a border whose guardians still required spontaneous Covid tests and a document providing contact information should one of those tests prove positive, was effortless and efficient. It was all accomplished from the driver's seat, and the guards freely offered their internet connection to find the appropriate forms to fill out. It was a fifty-five-mile drive, about an hour and a half, to Edessa and, again, the countryside was remarkably beautiful and wide open. This part of Northern Greece also is fruit-growing country, full of apple and plum orchards.

I detect a change in humidity as I drive down from the higher hills of North Macedonia. The road goes past Lake Vegoritis and over a series of ridges that must have given Roman roadbuilders much grief. I suspect the modern road is not quite the same route the Romans followed. The original Via

Egnatia is nearby—an early map tells me so—but it has been coyly hidden under an evolving landscape over the last millennium or so. I eventually follow a river with the fruit trees well behind me, and the landscape is opening up to limestone and scrub bushes, indicating I am getting closer to the Aegean Sea. There were marshes past this spot, and those Roman builders would have had to find a way over them as well.

This is watery country generally—streams, marshes, and the like all pushing toward Edessa. I was soon to discover how the geography of the landforms that ancient city sits on spectacularly handles all this water. Perhaps this aquatic condition adds to the warmer and damper feeling in the air as I sit outdoors at a small countryside eatery having lunch, and a more luxuriant vegetation all around me seems to thrive on it. I am glad I chose to stop in Edessa for a few days. It is at a midpoint between Bitola and Thessaloniki and offers ancient stones to wander around and natural watery features to visit.

An older book I consulted, Firmin O'Sullivan's *The Egnatian Way*, is a pleasant read but, published in 1972, is a bit outdated. I noticed what he noticed as soon as I drove into the city center, modern with postwar reconstruction. He wrote how the city sat on high cliffs. I walked to the edge after finding a legal place to park in the crowded downtown and caught what he caught, a whiff of the Aegean Sea, fewer than fifty miles to the southeast.

He gave me the name of what I was seeing from those cliffs "overlooking the valley of the Lydias," which friends I met there spelled as the Loudías Potamós (Potamós means river). The town, O'Sullivan said, from its marvelous height on those cliffs overlooks the Thessaloniki countryside. And below those cliffs sit ruins known as Loggos. The ancient town was built on two levels: the Roman forum was in the now-modern city above; homes, baths, and workshops were in what are now the ruins below.

O'Sullivan also gave me what previous generations had thought the city's earliest name was, the pre-Hellenic name Aigai. The modern name Edessa was also the ancient name, a word meaning "town on the water."

A local historian I met for coffee one afternoon, Makis Konidis, confirmed this early name, spelling it as Aiges. For centuries, he told me, folks thought Aiges had been, in the fourth century B.C., the capital of Macedonia. But in 1977, five years after O'Sullivan published his book—unknowingly citing the name misinformation—archaeologists discovered, at a place thirty-five miles south of Edessa called Vergina, a series of royal tombs of Macedonian leaders. This area included the final resting place of Alexander's father, who was murdered there in 336 B.C., dashing the long-held belief that Edessa started out as the Macedonia capital Aiges.

The Romans captured Edessa in 168 B.C. and, a few decades later, extended their road from the Adriatic coast through the ancient city and beyond to Thessaloniki, nearly sixty miles away. At some point after that—precise dating is not known— the road was pushed through to Byzantium.

Edessa in the medieval period was called Vodena, from the Slavic name Voda, which means "water." When the Ottoman Empire was on its way out, Vodena was annexed by Greece in 1912. Then, in 1923, its citizenry decided to take back the ancient name of Edessa.

I spent a full day wandering through the central business district of mostly postwar buildings. My hosts, Georgia Delimpanidou and George Raptis, told me that the Germans, in

September 1944, destroyed much of the city in retaliation for a rebel attack against them, hence the more modern buildings. They said there was an area, Varossi, on the far side of the town's soccer stadium and close to the edge of the cliffs that was all that remained from that destruction. My intentions were good. I wanted to go there. But time slipped away. My goal was to be as close to the Via Egnatia pathway as possible. It was in the center, not at Varossi. I promised myself I would get over there on another trip soon.

The Via Egnatia ran through the city, and in a large park it ran along the Edessaios River that courses its way through the town. Its origins are the Agra Nisi Vrytta Wetlands, located a few miles west of Edessa near the small village of Agras, a location on the Via Egnatia.

When the river reaches Edessa, there is a bridge over the waterway that is now bustling its way through a controlled channel. This structure gives a hint of the Egnatia's route that is buried under a modern city, but today no traffic goes over it. It provides a photogenic stone walkway over the Edessaios.

Apparently, there is disagreement over whether it is an original Roman bridge or one from the Byzantines. I suspect the Byzantines remodeled it from an existing Roman structure, molding it into a combination of both. Oldness seems to be respected here. Next to the bridge is a London plane tree that, according to a marker, is 350 years old, placing its planting in the 1670s, during the early centuries of the Ottoman Empire. A delight to inspect, admire, and respect.

I walked along the river's edge, across city streets, and toward the park where the river's water splits and tumbles over the edge of the plateau in a series of waterfalls. Also here is a trail down the cliffs that literature from the site indicates is the route of the Via Egnatia. It would be unusual for Roman road-builders to create such a steep route, but various guidebooks say this is where the road went. When it would reach the plain below, it ran along the edge of the Roman village there that locals call Loggos. I didn't walk down along what the guides say is the road. I admired the waterfalls. I have read different estimates about how many there are, but the composite number seems to be twelve. Most are hidden in the thick foliage, but four magnificent and powerful waterfalls are readily visible. Huge volumes of water pour over the cliff's face, and steps leading down alongside the larger ones offer a close look and lots of spray. The fall day I was there was quite warm. The spray was welcome.

I returned to my car and drove down and around the high plateau's edge to Loggos below. It is a marvelous collection of ruins. In the fifth and sixth centuries B.C., ancient Edessa developed in two places—one was high above on the plateau where the modern city sits. This was the area of the town's acropolis, or center, where today are scattered remains of its ancient fortifications. And below, on the plain, there are tombs and the remains of temples to various gods and goddesses, a typical Roman theater, plus what appear to archaeologists to be storage rooms, homes, and shops where craftsmen work.

When the Romans came in the second century B.C., they built the Via Egnatia through Edessa high on the cliff and through Loggos far below in what was then a large, wooded area. Their aim early in the history of the road was to make it to Thessaloniki and then pause. Edessa and Loggos were a perfect way station on that route.

Much of Loggos remains underground. On the eastern edge, an ancient gate pops up in a small clearing. It is open and allows visitors access to the site's boundary. But the trail up to the top of the modern hill ends in a cluster of undergrowth, a natural barrier blocking my way back toward the open area. Ruins underfoot on this spot have yet to be uncovered and tied to the main site to the west. Heading back to the aboveground ruins, I stop at the ticket office and get permission, for a few euros, to wander inside.

As I move along one of the set trails, a woman appears. She is there to answer visitor questions. Unfortunately, she speaks no English, and I speak no Greek. We quietly acknowledge each other, and she points out areas closed to visitors.

I see a spot where a theater was uncovered. A guidebook tells me that it was excavated and, for mysterious reasons, covered back up again. As a visitor over the years to dozens of archaeological sites and in conversations with archaeologists, I have learned that when money runs out, excavations cease. And important spots, such as a Roman theater, likely would be covered back up to preserve the site for the next generation of students of antiquity to explore.

I can see, standing on a high spot amid the ruins, a paved road running alongside the site's eastern edge. It would have to be the Egnatia route that a well-executed map I had in a guidebook said was there. I returned to my car, hoping to return on a more leisurely trip. Then I bid farewell to Loggos and headed to a very old monastery a short distance away. This is the Agia Triada monastery. One source calls it a nunnery. But this particular structure is relatively new, dating only to 1865. However, it was built on the ruins of a forerunner dating back to the Byzantine period and beyond.

And it was built alongside the Via Egnatia. More interesting to me was the discovery of the remains of a Roman bath and a milestone next to the church. This told me I was on the right track. I followed the road, knowing the ancient one was below me by perhaps six feet. Today it's a farm road running through fallow fields, connecting to a modern highway a mile or so away.

Beginning two thousand years ago, great Roman, Byzantine, and Ottoman armies, Goths and other invaders, and pilgrims walking to Constantinople trudged along its stones, and merchants used it up to the beginning of the twentieth century. Thessaloniki is just fifty miles away, a midpoint in the journey eastward or westward. Again, I felt the sense of discovery I experienced on that straight stretch of the Via Appia south of Rome to Terracina.

Late the next morning, I headed for the small village a few miles west of Edessa called Agras, site of the wetlands that feed the Edessaios River. My *Egnatian Way* guidebook recommends that those walking the roadway should find a train station outside of the town—next to that, with a shaded terrace, is a bar/restaurant—and the book gives specific instructions about where the proper route could be. Behind the station is a small bridge that joins a narrow dirt road leading to the town. Again, this is speculation, but it was the route offered for walkers to keep them as close to the Via Egnatia as possible, if not right on it. Toon Pennings (who is associated with the authors of the detailed guidebook I've been using) said in our correspondence about the road behind the train station that it is "impossible to say if that was Via Egnatia."

Either way, I needed to see it. The train station was closed—shut down for fifteen years according to the waiter at the bar/restaurant. I asked him about the bridge behind the station and, since I was the eatery's only patron, he walked with me to the spot. A small "bridge"—consisting only of a few wooden planks and quite shaky—lay across a stream. The dirt road was there. I thought that after lunch I might drive on it to see where it goes, but the waiter advised against it. The road becomes just a pathway, he said, too narrow for a car. We walked back, and I had a full Greek meal to carry me on to Pella, Alexander's birthplace. A few other diners eventually arrived, and the small restaurant got quite busy. It was justified. The food was excellent.

I was making a relatively short drive to Pella, site of the ruins of the palace of Philip II, Macedonia's eighteenth ruler. In addition to being the birthplace of his son, it also was where Alexander's half sister, Thessaloniki, for whom the city was named, was born. Here myth and reality collide. There are variations on the legend, but basically Thessaloniki accidentally drank the water of immortality and became a mermaid. After Alexander's death, she would swim out to greet ships and ask their crews if Alexander was alive. If they said he had died, she would sink the ship, drowning the sailors, and she then would create a great sea storm from her tears.

In reality, she married Cassander, a Macedonian king who did away with the name of the ancient city of Therma, a short distance to the southeast, and named it after her. Later, after Cassander's death, one of her sons, jealous over her perceived favoritism for a brother, had his mother killed.

The city of Thessaloniki sits prominently on the Aegean coast and is overflowing with two thousand or more years of history. I would be moving there the day after seeing Pella.

Pella is less than an hour east from Edessa, through open country and just off the Egnatia Odos. There are no orchards here, just large fields surrounding the site with cotton as the dominant crop. Someday, I imagine, if funds are plentiful, these fields will be taken apart and more tombs and structures—Macedonian, Greek, and Roman—will emerge. But for now, it is all about cotton. In the town between the site and the archaeological museum, many trucks used to harvest and haul the cotton to market sit empty along side streets waiting for the next growing season, white bits of cotton stuck in the metal framework.

Here, the Egnatia route is just a few miles north of the modern road and would have run through, or around, Pella, which now is a very large ruin. There are two main roads clearly demarcated—one north-south, another east-west—meeting at an intersection in the middle. The agora, an open meeting ground where citizens could gather, which is downhill from the remains of the palace, is seventy-five thousand square feet. There are some columns remaining, but the archaeological site is mostly level.

I first went to the museum on the edge of the modern town of Pella. It is a sophisticated facility with exhibits that tell stories rather than just display dusty bits of pottery and a few suits of battle gear and weapons. I was especially drawn to the room where stunningly preserved mosaics are presented. These are mosaics from Greek and Roman structures that once stood tall in the ancient city. Two sets particularly captured my attention. One floor display is from the House of Dionysus, showing a brilliantly composed picture made of tiny colored pieces of stone of the god Dionysus riding on the back of a panther. There are male and female unicorns as well. Another display of a stag hunt and beautifully depicted fauna is from the House of the Abduction of Helen, referring to the abduction that triggered the ten-year siege of Troy. I knew that the remains of the Diana house are roofed over at the archaeological site. The House of Dionysus floor is exposed with no protection from the elements.

I drove back through the village and down to the road leading to the archaeological site. My museum ticket also covered entrance there. After a short walk past open blocks where houses and shops once stood, I came to the House of Dionysus. The layout of rooms is difficult to imagine with no walls. This spot is named for the Greek god of fertility and wine; he was the mythological creator of wine. His father was Zeus, and his mother was a mortal who was killed by Zeus's wife, Hera, in a jealous rage. Dionysus was not yet born, and Zeus retrieved his unborn son from the mother's body and attached it to his hip to nurture it until he could be born.

Farther along was the House of the Abduction of Helen, protected by a wooden roof. Many of its mosaics remain. The stag hunt mosaic, now preserved in the museum, came from this fourth century B.C. house. It took me back to my memories of the goddess Diana from Nemi, south of Rome. Diana is the Roman version of the Greek goddess Artemis, the virginal huntress. Legend has it that a poor fellow named Actaeon happened upon Artemis while she was bathing nude, and she was so enraged she turned him into a stag. Then Actaeon's own dogs devoured him, not recognizing their master. In a rare, modern reference to this myth, Actaeon is depicted with Diana in the royal park back in Caserta, Italy.

Seeing these mosaics—both in the museum and at the site itself—was the highlight of my visit. The house names are from Greek myths. They were probably occupied by very rich Macedonians and, later, Romans. I imagine the names were attached closer to modern times based on the subjects of the mosaics.

There is no indication that the Via Egnatia went through the site. I observed the main roads and wondered if one of them could be it, but an archaeologist in Thessaloniki two days later said he does not believe that it went directly through either Pella or his city. The gates would be closed at night, and whole armies could not be allowed in the city as they were transiting through the countryside. After all, when the Via Egnatia was built it was a military road and not just anybody could use it. It would be too disruptive to city life to house an encampment of soldiers. So, the main "highway" would go around. This is not true for all cities in the classical period. Beyond Thessaloniki, for example, is ancient Philippi, and the Via Egnatia is clearly the main road through that ruin. Without an understanding of where that small segment of the Egnatia at Pella is, I must accept that it was built nearby, but outside the city's walls. At some point, it would have dropped down and flowed eastward, either beneath or directly on a parallel course with the modern Egnatia Odos.

I arrived in Thessaloniki late that afternoon. The modern city, pleasant enough in building designs and open spaces along the seafront, was jammed with automobiles, trucks, and buses. It took an hour from when I entered the city to when I found the street where my lodgings were located on a side street just off the waterfront. The narrow, one-way street was lined with cars parked on both sides. I passed the door of my new place and, a few feet farther along, I spotted an underground parking garage. Two men stood outside. I pulled up and they waved me away, saying they were full. "Come back in the morning," one of them said. But I need a place now, I indicated, shrugging and gesturing with my hands, palms up. Sorry, sorry. I moved on and decided to drive around the block, hoping a parking spot would immediately jump out at me. No such luck.

Fifteen minutes later, I was back on my street. I tried the garage again. "No, no, I told you, no places." But people will be leaving. Can I wait at the side? "No, you will block cars." He waved me on. Around again I went, two more times. It was the same story. The attendant, a young man in his late twenties, grew exasperated. Finally, on the fifth try, an older man, his partner, motioned me over to park in the driveway. He spoke some English. "You impress me with your determination," he said. "You can stay. Give us your keys, but you cannot leave for two days. If you do, you might lose your spot. We are full all the time. You will be parked in a place not easy to get out of." I agreed. I would be in Thessaloniki for three days and knew I could ride buses, take a taxi, or walk. It is a beautiful city, and the archaeological museum and small cluster of Roman ruins were close by. I agreed, paid in advance, and gave both men generous tips. We immediately became close friends.

My first plan was to wander the part of the city around my small apartment. That evening, after resting up from a long day of walking through ancient ruins, a drive to my next city, and spending more than an hour trying to negotiate a parking spot, I took a long walk toward the heart of Thessaloniki. I saw, on a sign, the name of the second two-way street I crossed. It said EGNATIA. It ran east and west through the heart of the city, but it did not fit with what I knew about the ancient road's route. I suspected it was a name given in honor of that 2,150-year-old route, with no expectation that the modern street followed it.

The next morning, I got my answer. I walked to the archaeological museum, bought my ticket, and asked the clerk if there was anyone who was knowledgeable about how the road related to the city. She pointed to a man sitting at the end of a long table surrounded by stacks of books. "He knows," she said, and she motioned him over. Haris Tsougaris is a staff archaeologist at the museum. We found a quiet corner on the edge of the reception area with a pair of comfortable chairs and talked about the Via Egnatia.

Haris emphasized that the Egnatia street through the city was certainly not the ancient route. He said ancient Thessaloniki was a walled city, and armies traveling along the Via Egnatia would not enter the gates, which were closed at night. Therefore, the Via Egnatia, when it reached the western gate, known as the Golden Gate near Vardaris Square, would make a sharp turn and run a course up and around the city.

Haris said that Pella, where I had been the day before and where I was frustrated by the fact that I could find no evidence of the road, also did not have the Via Egnatia run through its agora and forum areas. Instead, the road would stop at the gates and go around that city as well. The mystery was solved.

"Remember, it was a military road and, during the Roman period, was closed to commercial travel," he said. Ancient armies had to camp outside. Archaeologists found a milestone less than a mile to the north of Thessaloniki. It was discovered at a gate of a military barracks named for Pavlos Melas, a Greek hero who died fighting the Bulgarians in 1904. The milestone is written in Greek, he said, and "bears the names of Diocletian and various consequent Caesars . . . from [A.D.] 284 to 306.

"These discoveries allow us to trace the route. There are two small lakes [Volvi and Koroneia, also known as Langadas,] along this route, and the Egnatia ran between them and the city's upper limits," he told me. From there, it drops down and leads to the archaeological site of Philippi and beyond to

Neapolis, which today is Kavala, a distance from Thessaloniki of one hundred miles.

Haris told me that I need to see the Roman ruins near the center of the city just a short walk from the museum. He also recommended that I did not need to drive to the northern part of the city's edge to see if I could discern the precise Egnatia route. "It is covered, hidden," he said. "We have tried to trace short sections of the route, without success." He excused himself, saying he must get back to his work. It was a short but satisfying visit.

I walked to the ruins, which primarily consist of the Roman Forum of Thessaloniki. A comfortable bar on the forum's eastern edge provided a double caffè and a cream-filled cornetto. It also provided an outdoor table overlooking the Roman ruin, which I discovered was closed. A team of archaeologists and their helpers were down on the forum floor, well below street level. There are two terraces, both covered with columns supporting the roof. There are baths there, but I could not see them from my vantage point. A small theater has also been uncovered. Further reading told me that the theater and the forum were used until the sixth century A.D., then left to disappear beneath the demesne of a growing city's rulers. Answers to questions are generally easy to come by, but I sometimes had lousy luck finding places that were open when I traveled long distances to see them. This was one of those moments.

I understood that this forum was dug up by accident in the mid-twentieth century. Developers were planning to build a courthouse on the spot, but plans shifted when the ruins were uncovered. Today, a pleasant park sits to the south. Beyond, the main street is ironically the one called Egnatia. I later learned that this main west-east road through the heart of the city was widened in 1917 and given that name following a great fire.

Away from the south edge of the Ancient Agora and toward the sea is Aristotelous Square. The modern, architecturally interesting multistory buildings feature, at ground level, stoas, or covered walkways across their individual fronts. I admired the thoughtful contrast with these public walkways lined with shops, restaurants, and coffee bars to the roofed shelters uncovered in the Roman Forum. It is a concept found in ancient Greek architecture that was adapted by the Romans and now by modern architects set on transforming a major city center.

I spent a lot of time in that square sitting on convenient benches facing the Aegean Sea, watching commercial ships lining up to enter or exit Thessaloniki's busy port. With very little to see of the ancient road in this city—and with the forum closed—I decided to spend my last two days relaxing and researching this warm, friendly, beautiful place.

With Egypt far away across the Aegean and by extension the Mediterranean, I thought of Pompey escaping Caesar's army after the crushing, decisive defeat at Pharsalus 120 miles to the southwest and hiding out somewhere near my vantage point next to the lime-green sea. From here, he and his family caught passage to Egypt where, as soon as he disembarked at Pelusium, across the Nile delta from Alexandria, he was murdered on the orders of Ptolemy XIII, who was anxious to curry favor with Caesar. Instead, Ptolemy died in battle shortly thereafter, and victorious Caesar curried favor with his sister, Cleopatra.

12

FROM PHILIPPI TO BYZANTIUM AND BACK TO THE BOOT

So Philippi again saw Roman armies clash
amongst themselves, with equal weapons:
And the gods thought it not unfitting
that Emathia and the broad plain
of Haemus, should twice be enriched with our blood.
And a time will come, when in those lands,
the farmer labouring at the earth with curved plough,
will come upon spears eaten by scabrous rust,
or strike an empty helmet with his heavy hoe,
and wonder at giant bones in the opened grave.

—Roman poet Virgil

I handed my car park ticket to one of my new Thessalonian friends, and he disappeared down a steep concrete driveway into the bowels of the parking structure to retrieve my car. It was day three of my time in Thessaloniki. I was anxious to get to the ruins of Philippi and relive the battles on the plain near the Pangaion Hills. Near to Philippi is the coastal town of Kavala, which in ancient times was called Neapolis. I would stay there for a few days of extensive exploring of Philippi. It would be my last stop in Greece before heading over the Turkish border to Istanbul. Neapolis was part of ancient Thracia, a Roman province that included the European part of Turkey.

It was at Philippi that the Via Egnatia pushed through its heart and, by connecting with Neapolis on the Aegean Sea, it provided a pathway for armies and Christian apostles disembarking at the port and then moving along the staunchly built Roman road on their way west to connect with the city of Philippians. This was the land that the poet Virgil wrote about in book 1 of *The Georgics,* a collection of poems he wrote to educate farmers about how to plow fields and anticipate weather. Here, he said, on the large plain before the city of Philippi, was the famous, epoch-turning battlefield where the history of the Western world forever shifted on a warm October day in 42 B.C. Farmers for generations to come would likely plow up buried instruments of war.

I first went to my hillside lodgings in Kavala, finding a comfortable apartment with a view (if I turned a certain way) of the Aegean Sea far below. I was on the town's western edge; Neapolis would have been built up along the shoreline and hillside on the eastern edge. I had a couple of days here before moving on to Turkey, nearly 120 miles away. I expected I would spend at least two days at the archaeological site at Philippi, a quick nine-mile drive, along a highway called Ethniki Odos, into the hills above.

The next day was spent at Philippi. This archaeological site is one of the more impressive plots I have ever visited. It is well organized and staffed. There are a couple of shops and a few places to eat. The parking lot was nearly empty. I suspect tourism was down because of the strict Covid rules within Greece. I was just thankful the site was open.

The place is more than one thousand feet above sea level, and the ancient town offers sweeping views of the coastal plain. The plain was occupied by various Thracian tribes until 360 B.C. when settlers from the Greek island of Thasos came. They founded a seaport village and called it Datos or Datum, whose location is lost. A short four years later, Alexander's father, the Macedonian king Philip II, came, saw, and conquered. And he founded Philippi farther inland, naming it after himself. He was interested in mining gold from the nearby Pangaion Hills. It made him rich. Philip enlarged and fortified the town, probably building the first semicircular theater in the hillside. When the Romans came in, around 160 B.C., they set about improving the theater to hold eight thousand spectators, and they expanded the forum.

Of course, those Romans then ran the Via Egnatia right through the city, unlike in Pella and Thessaloniki, places where the road was routed around. It was this road, coming in from the west or the segment that connected the port of Neapolis to Philippi nine miles away, that the Romans followed, with armies from both sides, to their eventual and history-shifting Battle of Philippi, in 42 B.C.

Octavian and Antony arrived at different times and from different directions. Antony likely disembarked from ships at Neapolis; Octavian, who had been delayed with sickness at the port of Dyrrachium far to the west, probably came overland. From either direction, they trudged along the road to that fateful town. On the plain, they clashed with armies made up of fellow Romans, the armies of two men who had conspired with others to kill Caesar nineteen months earlier.

Brutus and Cassius had been in the east raising armies and

hoping to eventually push Octavian and Antony out of the picture and ensure the republic would survive. They were already nearby. The first battle was on October 3. It pitted the army of Mark Antony against that of Cassius. Cassius had the edge but did not know it. Each army had captured the other's camp. He had received an erroneous report that the battle was lost. He ordered his servant to kill him. The armies of Antony, Octavian, and their remaining opponent, Brutus, waited twenty days. When fighting resumed on October 23, Brutus lost the edge. Sensing defeat, he, too, sought death. Ironically, the man he and Cassius helped murder, Julius Caesar, had once written that men committing suicide were making "unduly harsh plans about their lives."

I like the way Shakespeare ended his play *Julius Caesar*. Antony calls Brutus "the noblest Roman of them all," because unlike the other conspirators who killed "the great Caesar" out of envy, only Brutus did it for a noble cause, the preservation of the republic. Then Octavian, who within fifteen years would be declared emperor, speaks:

> *According to his virtue let us use him,*
> *With all respect and rites of burial.*
> *Within my tent his bones to-night shall lie,*
> *Most like a soldier, order'd honorably.*
> *So call the field to rest, and let's away.*
> *To part the glories of this happy day.*

I stood on top of a wall just above the section of Via Egnatia that runs through the ruins at the base of the theater carved out of the hillside and looked out over the plain where many thousands of Romans killed one another. Generously, when Octavian and Antony declared victory and took unchallenged control of the soon-to-be empire, they forgave the surrendering soldiers from the other side. Antony later established a settlement for ex-legionnaires at Philippi.

I ran into a park guide, Alexandros Lamprianidis, who shared with me his knowledge about the battle and the Roman city. He pointed up to the top of the mountain, far above the theater, saying that Cassius, on horseback, watched that first battle from there and got the incorrect message that his side was losing.

Later in our walk, Alexandros showed me the small cell where legend has it that the apostle Paul and his companion Silas had been imprisoned. The legend says that an earthquake knocked the cell door open, allowing the men to leave. But before taking off toward Thessaloniki, they baptized a few folks, including, according to what may be a literary invention by Luke the Evangelist, a woman trader named Lydia of Thyatira, an ancient Greek city in what is now Asian Turkey. She is described as non-Jewish but friendly toward Judaism. And Paul may also have converted the jailer and his family. Some scholars suggest that Paul made two trips to Philippi ten years apart. Eventually, Paul would end up in Italy, first landing in Malta, then Sicily, and finally disembarking, under Roman guard, at Puteoli, today's Pozzuoli, a few miles north of Naples. He, along with Saint Luke, would be taken to Rome, traveling along the Via Appia.

We walked across the wide forum whose construction began in Macedonian times and later was expanded by the Romans. There, near its eastern edge, were the ruins of an octagonal basilica that was dedicated to Saint Paul. The ruins of a couple of other basilicas are there as well. After the Western Roman Empire ended in the late fifth century A.D., Philippi remained an important part of the Eastern Roman Empire ruled by the Byzantines out of Constantinople. Around the seventh century, the city was in great decline, particularly after an earthquake that devastated the area in 619. Its shattered ruins became a Byzantine garrison for a while. But after 1453, when the Ottomans took over the empire by conquering Constantinople, Philippi ceased to be inhabited.

Paul certainly wrote about his visits to this area. Saint Peter likely trod these stones and the stones of the Via Appia far to the west, as well.

There was a message awaiting me when I returned to my apartment. A friend of a friend had found a guide to show me segments of the Via Egnatia on the edge of Kavala and along the route to Philippi. This was fortunate. Haris Tsougaris in Thessaloniki had given me a few directions to possible sites near Kavala, but my solitary search led nowhere. Now I had a guide who could take me to spots that are not listed in any of the guidebooks I consulted.

I exchanged messages with Soula Tsolaki. We agreed to meet the next morning at the Holy Church of Saint Nicholas. This was near the waterfront on Kavala's eastern edge, on the spot where the ancient city of Neapolis now lay under paved streets and modern buildings.

I arrived early and got a caffè from a shop across the street from the church. There was a large stone mural in front of the imposing but beautifully appointed structure with warm Mediterranean hues of yellow and white that indicated this was the spot where Saint Paul, on his missionary pilgrimage to Philippi during the winter of A.D. 49, first stepped on European soil. The sea, which the shop owner indicated bordered this area, had been much closer. Now, two thousand years later, it was a handful of blocks to the south. From here, Paul and his companion Silas and perhaps others stepped onto the Via Egnatia en route to Philippi a dozen miles away.

The church building dates to the sixteenth century, when the Ottomans ruled this part of the Mediterranean. Therefore, it was first a mosque. It became a Christian church in 1926 after the Ottoman Empire finally collapsed, and, in 1945, it was named for Saint Nicholas, patron of sailors. I wondered why this church, on the spot where Saint Luke landed, was named for another saint, Agios Nikolaos, who, in the third and fourth centuries, gave gifts to the poor and became the modern model for Santa Claus.

Apparently, Soula Tsolaki told me after she arrived and joined me for caffè, this church was built on top of an early Christian basilica that likely was dedicated to Saint Paul. Further reading indicates that there are remains of this original structure placed in the bema, the raised part of an Eastern church that contains the altar. The altar in the Church of Saint Nicholas is dedicated to Saint Paul.

Soula said the origins of Neapolis go back to the seventh century B.C. And, surrounded by its defensive wall, the city was limited to the hill that rose up to the east of the church. As recently as 1864, modern Kavala began to develop westward, along the seafront.

We drove to the western edge of Kavala near the neighborhood where I was staying. We passed a small two-table restaurant where I had eaten a wonderful Greek lunch the day before, not knowing how close I was to the route of the ancient road.

The drive took us up a small hill on a paved road and when the pavement stopped we parked and started walking. Within a few dozen feet we were on old Roman stones. This was the Via Egnatia, uncovered decades ago. Soula told me that in

1934, people from the Greek University of Salonica, now Aristotle University of Thessaloniki, started to excavate the road and identified it as the Via Egnatia. About five or six years ago, she said some historians began to question whether it was that road. They speculated that it was a Turkish road built in the sixteenth century. Signs identifying it as the Via Egnatia were taken down. But that speculation has been officially dismissed, she said. The signs have gone back up.

This ancient road was built with local materials, ranging from one to four layers of cobblestones. Clay soil made up some layers, particularly in soft or damp soil. Up until the early twentieth century, this narrow road was busy with farmers' carts and horses. It was the only way into and out of Kavala until modern times. Over time, highways were built, and the Egnatia was left to deteriorate and, in some sections, to disappear under pavement.

It was a wonderful find for me. We did not walk the entire length that has been uncovered, slightly less than a mile long; it would have taken us to the modern highway on which I traveled into and out of Kavala. The end of this segment disappears under the highway and then, hidden, follows the path under a secondary road, the Ethniki Odos, which leads to Philippi.

Come, Soula indicated as we trudged back down those old stones to the car. "We have more to see." We drove up to the highway and turned onto the Ethniki Odos. After a short drive, we turned off at a wide spot and stopped. Here, the stones reappeared. Only these glistened in the sunlight, and the full width of the road had been carefully excavated. In contrast to the segment we just left, crews were uncovering this section that was revealing itself almost before our eyes. It was being performed under the supervision of an archaeologist from the Hellenic

Ministry of Culture. Tools were neatly stacked, and no one was on the job. It was a national holiday. She said workers would be back the next day.

Again, we went for a walk. The still-buried pathway behind us came down a hillside where Saint Paul and Saint Silas had stopped for a night on their three-day walk to Philippi. Near the top is a monastery built in 1936 and dedicated to Saint Silas. Here, restoration on the road began and is heading slightly downhill toward the plain of Philippi where the battles were fought that led to a victorious Octavian eventually becoming Rome's first emperor.

The exposed road is about the same length as the section we had walked on back in Kavala, slightly less than a mile. This time, we walked to where labor had ended the day before. Beyond were farmer's fields; there was no trace of a road under trees and high grass. Virgil's poem flashed through my mind, and I thought about farmers who, while tilling those fields that stretch across this once brutal plain, "will come upon spears eaten by scabrous rust, or strike an empty helmet with his heavy hoe, and wonder at giant bones in the opened grave."

I am leaving Philippi/Kavala feeling a great deal of pleasure, thanks to my guide Soula Tsolaki. To experience those stones of the Via Egnatia for good walking distances was deeply satisfying. I now needed to head for Kipoi, Greece, at the border with Turkey, find a safe place to park my car for three days, meet my cross-border driver, Ahmet, and then hook up, in Keşan, with my Turkish friend and professional guide, Lütfi Baydar.

I had my required documents: passport, CDC Covid vaccination card, and itinerary in Turkey with my phone number in case the Covid test at the border showed positive. Kipoi was not far, an easy two-hour drive along the Egnatia Odos (E90). This route likely covers a significant portion of the ancient road and then, as it gets closer to the Turkish border, runs parallel with the Via Egnatia located slightly closer to the coastline. I decided to stay on the E90 and not drift off because I had to be in Kipoi by a certain time to meet the Turkish driver, Ahmet Gökhan Kahyağlu, and I did not have any idea how long it would take me to find a spot for my car. I pressed on along the modern road, enjoying the mountains to my left and the Aegean on my right.

There are a lot of warnings that a border crossing is ahead. Hundreds—perhaps the number is more than a thousand—of semitrailer trucks are in line, parked alongside the road, awaiting their turn at customs. I pass the end of the line six or seven miles out and long before I see evidence of the border station ahead. The wait for these drivers must be hours. Occasionally there were gaps where trucks had moved forward and the driver in the vehicle behind must have fallen asleep. No one tries to get ahead by crowding into the wide-open spaces. They were used to it I suspect and civilized about the process.

Lütfi had told me I could park in the lot next to a small café just before the Greek part of the border station. I got there and the lot was completely full. I drove around in a circle and passed it again and again. No spot had opened. Off to the side, I saw an information trailer. I stopped, went to the window, and found a clerk who spoke excellent English. He understood my problem. "Do not go there," he said of the café lot. "It will be futile. Instead, go back a mile in the direction you came, but do not get on the E90. Take the side road just ahead. There will be a gasoline station. You can ask to park there."

Whew. I did as he directed. The gasoline station had a bar. I went in, ordered a double caffè, and asked the young woman if it was possible to park. She understood English and pointed to the station owner, who had just walked in. She asked him in Greek, he looked at me, smiled broadly, threw up his arms, and said what I assume was the loud, friendly equivalent of "Of course! No problem." There was a covered parking structure to the side. "There!" he said, putting his arm around my shoulder and leading me outside. "For three days?" I asked. She translated his answer. "As long as you like."

I parked and pulled out one bag, leaving the other one in the trunk. For some reason, I just knew it would be safe. Sitting down with the caffè, I messaged Ahmet and gave him directions. Within forty-five minutes, time enough for me to unwind after the confusion at the border, my new driver friend pulled into the station. Thirty minutes later, Ahmet and I were across the border and heading to Keşan, passing a reverse lineup of semitrailers waiting to enter Greece, also at least six or seven miles long.

Lütfi had an itinerary planned for our drive to Istanbul. Turkey is not known for preserving any sections of the Via Egnatia. In my early research I could not find any references to uncovered sections. Lütfi had studied sources about the road that were published in Turkish and had an idea where we might find a segment or two and, perhaps, a fifteenth-century bridge on the spot where a Roman bridge might have carried a piece of the road over a stream.

We went through two small villages, Ahmetçe and Oğuzlu, each with their own small mosques. Lütfi talked to folks in three different locations: a dairy farmer, elderly men sitting in the sun, a man cutting firewood. None knew the location of an old stone bridge dating back that far. Bridgeless, we headed back toward Keşan. Lütfi knew of another possible location of a road segment, and we soon were following a road through a marshy area. We went past a small lake. There, alongside the road, we found a shepherd with his flock. "Is this the old road through the Balkans," Lütfi asked the man. He directed us to go back a short distance, turn, and drive across a wooden bridge over an irrigation canal. At the turn, we found another man who directed us farther along. A small, very rough dirt road greeted us. After a short drive, it split off with another road, virtually impassible with mud. We pressed on following the original road until it, too, became impassible. A short walk convinced us we were not on the right road. We concluded that the road to the spot where we understood a short segment of the Via Egnatia to be was the first muddy, undrivable one.

The sun was low. There were only a few hours of daylight left. We had to give up. That segment is out there, and we were probably less than a mile from it. But getting stuck in the muddy wetlands was not something we wanted to experience. We got back to the paved highway, reached Keşan, and turned east toward Istanbul, three and a half hours away.

At least we had the satisfaction of knowing that by following E84/E80 to that glorious city on the Bosphorus, we were following much of the route of the now well-hidden Via Egnatia. Some sources I found reveal that the ancient Roman route corresponded with the name the early Ottomans gave it— Rumeli Sol Kol, or Balkan Left Arm—and went from Keşan to the coast of the Sea of Marmara at Tekirdağ, then along the coast to Istanbul. The Ottomans had created a triple main road system. The "left arm" reference refers to the ancient Roman route I have been following. There also are "middle arm" and "right arm" roads through different sections of Asian Turkey.

We were scheduled to spend only a few days in Istanbul, a city I was somewhat familiar with from two previous visits. Lütfi had been my group's guide on the second visit, during which we had limited time. That is where our friendship began. The highlights of that trip were visits to Hagia Sophia and the Blue Mosque. The Hagia Sophia was a Christian church ordered built by the Byzantine emperor Justinian I in the sixth century. It was built on the site of earlier Christian churches with the original ordered by Constantine, who wanted it built on the foundations of a pagan temple.

Earthquakes and fires had destroyed those earlier churches, but when Justinian ordered a new one built, the magnificent Hagia Sophia arose from those ashes in just six years. Under the Ottomans a millennium later, it became a mosque. In 1934, Turkish president Mustafa Kemal Atatürk secularized the building and turned it into a museum. That was its status during my first two visits. Then, in 2020, a year before my third trip, it was turned back into a mosque.

The line to enter the Hagia Sophia, despite it being amid the Covid pandemic, was long. I wanted to see the interior. Fully masked and vaccinated—twice and with a booster—I got in line and followed it into a crowded interior. I did not need to wander into the great hall with its spectacular Christian murals, left intact even in its transformation into a mosque. People were packed in there elbow to elbow. I stood in the doorway, took in the scene, and left, finding Lütfi over by the exit doors.

He was eager to show me something. We walked a few

dozen feet across the tram tracks and, out of sight behind a high steel-paneled fence, was the remains of a monument that Lütfi said had been known for nearly two thousand years as the Milion Stone. I had not heard of this before, despite earlier readings in preparation for my trip. The word *milion* was the Greek spelling; it can be spelled with two *l*s, but it has nothing to do with the number we see in English. Apparently, a *milion* is a type of ancient Roman monument, with a gate on each of the four sides, generally built on a crossroads. This stone, said Lütfi, marked the end of the Via Egnatia, or as it was known during the Ottoman Empire, Sol Kol, or Left Arm. Lütfi told me that folks in Istanbul still refer to the route through the modern city, from the Golden Gate just five miles away to the Milion Stone, as the Left Arm.

I had to keep in mind that the Milion Stone we see today is a faint remnant of what once stood here. The stone could be what remains of one of the four columns that formed four arches holding up a dome. Reportedly there would have been statues of Constantine and his mother, Helena, along with one of a goddess who was important to the city. Over time, the monument gained in grandeur as statues of subsequent emperors and their families were added.

When the Ottomans took the city in 1453, the site gradually declined and ultimately disappeared. It was not until the 1960s that pieces of what authorities believed were the monument started turning up buried and repurposed in the foundations of old medieval houses that were being torn up. The column we see today was salvaged from all that confusion and re-erected to honor the memory of what was once here.

The Egnatia route through the city to this stone tower, which we could not see because of the fencing that surrounded crews doing archaeological explorations and restoration work, was obvious. We could easily follow the main streets that make up the direct route to the Golden Gate. But the dilemma was how could we see the Milion Stone? We wandered around the outside of the enclosure. It appeared locked up solid. A restaurant lined one side. A kind gentleman running it allowed me to stand up on a bench and look over the fenced enclosure. I could see, through heavy branches of trees, the tall brick tower that marked the spot, but the smaller tower, the Milion Stone, was out of view. We thanked the man, promised we would return for dinner—a promise I was glad I kept because the food was wonderful—and went back to the busy street.

It was then I noticed two men at the wall who were working on a partially opened panel. We went down but got there just as they had closed the panel and were welding it shut. Lütfi asked if it was possible to get inside some other way. One of the welders suggested we go to the project office at a gate on the far side of the enclosure. "Ask," he said. We did. A couple of engineers were in the office. When they heard what we wanted, we got immediate permission. One of them unlocked the gate leading into the site. "Be careful," we were admonished. The site was crisscrossed with wooden planks laid over the labyrinth of low stone walls surrounding open spaces. It looked as if there were ancient rooms that had been buried underground and now were exposed. We started across a short wooden walkway and there it was, the Milion Stone. This weathered, indomitable piece of granite was first ordered erected by Constantine in the fourth century when he came to Byzantium, which he had renamed New Rome. It stood at the entrance of the Basilica Cistern and originally was part of a Roman forum with arches and stone columns.

Now, it stands with its base far below the rough construction planking used by workers. Before this project started and the site had been open to the public, there was an enduring walkway surrounding the stone to allow tourists to get up close. The stone itself was encased within a glass screen to keep thousands of tourists' hands off its restored surface. And, since the stone was placed there to mark a starting point for roads leading to the breadth of the Roman—and later Byzantine—Empires, tourists were able to see the distances, printed on walkway panels, from the stone to cities all over Asia and Europe. I suspect that kind of helpful information will be returned to the site when the restoration work is done.

Our visit was short. We had promised the man in the office we would make it quick. But we got close enough for me to say I had reached the end of the Via Egnatia. I did not want to get so close that I would be tempted to touch the stone now exposed to the elements; my sensitivities about not touching historic objects in museums bled through on this dusty restoration site.

My journey had begun in Rome nearly three months earlier following the famed Via Appia and continued through the Balkans on another major road to a city that marked its end. My only regret was missing the pandemic-stymied route through Albania. Slowly, Lütfi and I made our way across the planks leading to the exit, waving goodbye to the man inside the office, and dropped down into the bustle of people and vehicles outside the temporary wall.

The next day, we decided, would include a walk along the main street, the Left Arm, toward the Golden Gate through which emperors rode in grand processions, high on horseback or in glamorous wheeled carts, on the Via Egnatia and entered the city. For now, it was dinnertime, and I had that promise to keep.

In ancient times, the route of the Via Egnatia from the Golden Gate at the city walls to the Milion Stone monument was called the Mese. It reportedly had a marble surface and was decorated with marble columns and a portico lined with shops at street level and sculptures on the upper floors. Today, this route is made up of a sequence of three modern roads, laid out in succession, and it cuts a traffic-heavy swath through the city's center. My friend and I decided to walk a brief stretch, now of course much wider than the ancient road, and with modern stores, Turkish baths, and university buildings lining it. The sidewalks were full of people in the heat of the day. A short distance to the west of the Milion Stone, the Roman emperor Theodosius I had built a forum in the late fourth century. Also built there was the Arch of Theodosius, a triple triumphal arch with statues of the emperor and two of his sons, Arcadius and Honorius.

Lütfi and I, walking west, came upon what is left of the arch. Only a partial support for one side remains, and it sits on the edge of the sidewalk full of students and shoppers. Other than this arch and the remains of a Roman column dedicated to Constantine, there is not much to indicate this neighborhood's past. We visited a small museum with ancient stones under glass next to a modern building and then walked back toward the Milion Stone.

We took a taxi and drove out of the city, toward the western gate a few miles away where the Via Egnatia entered through the Golden Gate. The driver knew precisely where we wanted to go and agreed to wait as we headed toward an enclosed area with the gate beyond. There was construction work going on, restoring portions of the city's old walls. As we headed into the compound, which when open was a gathering spot for tourists, we were stopped by a construction worker who appeared to be a boss. "This is closed," he said brusquely. "You cannot go in."

Lütfi said we only wanted to see the Golden Gate and would be just a few minutes. But unlike the cooperative boss at the Milion Stone site, this man would not yield. We turned around, and he locked the gate behind us. That was that. We were leaving the next day for the Greek border and the beginning of my journey back to Rome. "We have to drive by here on the way to the border," Lütfi said. "We will try again."

We did try again and this time found the small construction gate wide open. No boss in sight. We simply walked through and into the compound surrounded by magnificent stone walls. Scaffolding dominated the areas around the gate and along the walls where workers could be seen restoring them. Ahead was the Golden Gate with a lesser gate on its left side. It is obvious that the original gate was once high and magnificent. Now, that grand opening has been filled with brick, with a much smaller entrance left open several feet below where the high point of the gate was once.

Roman and Byzantine emperors used this gate to make glorious entrances and follow the route to the Milion Stone five miles east. At this gate was the beginning of the main street we had walked along the day before, the Mese, the pathway known by a variety of modern names. Of course, Mese replaced the Via Egnatia name, and stones, partially restored, were in plain view through this parklike area, used for music events and outdoor theatricals—when there is no construction going on.

Whether the stones we were walking on were laid by the Romans or augmented over the centuries, we could not tell. We found a bench, sat for a while undisturbed by a construction boss, and imagined what this place would have looked like in the fourth century and later with all those triumphal processionals led by emperors and kings.

Then, it was time. We had a three-hour return drive to the border where I would meet Ahmet for the trip across and another Covid test administered by customs officials with friendly eyes showing above their masks. With the Bosphorus behind me and the Sea of Marmara to my left, we headed west—a general direction I would not deviate from until I reached Rome. There would be additional sights to see on the roads back, but at this point I had made it, with the brief exception of Albania, along two old Roman highways tying together east and west and built in the days just after the people of Rome had climbed down from their small hillside homes and gone on to create an empire that changed the course of Western history forever.

13

NEARING THE END

Now Ordona, about twelve miles to the east of
Aeca, now Troja, Livy records the defeat of the
Roman forces at this place in two successive
years. Hannibal removed the inhabitants
and fired the town, but it was subsequently repaired,
and is noticed by Frontinus as Ardona.
Ptolemy and Silius Italicus, mention it as Herdonia.

—Strabo

A part from Albania, I have traveled the length of two Roman roads—the Via Appia in Italy and the Via Egnatia across the Balkans. During my pre-Balkans visit in Brindisi, I went up along the southern portions of the Via Traiana route, along the Adriatic coast as far north as the archaeological ruins of Horace's Gnatia.

Now I need to slowly make my way to Rome and my return flight, but I still have time near the end of my three-month sojourn. The decision about the route back north seemed obvious. I would drive the entire length of the Via Traiana from Brindisi to Bari, then divert briefly to the north and visit the ancient battlefield at Cannae. I would return to the Via

Traiana at the small village of Ascoli Satriano and on to Troia, where the road passes through its old town.

There are things to see around Troia, so I will spend a few days there and on to Benevento where the faster Traiana route diverged from the slower, hillier Via Appia. The roads divided at one of the more magnificent arches left over from ancient Rome, the Arch of Trajan, which was completed the year of his death in 117 A.D. I had bypassed entering Benevento proper on my initial journey, telling myself I would spend time there on my return trip. Now was the time.

After settling in Bari for a quick two-day walking visit—I had found a no-pay parking spot in a very crowded lot a short distance away that I did not want to give up—I went two blocks east of my main street lodgings and found a gratifying view eastward across the Adriatic with Albania calling me from a distance. I could not see that elusive place, of course, but my pandemic-inspired frustrations overflowed. Maybe the pandemic restriction had been lifted I thought, and I could jump on a new ferry and go across for a quick day or so. Not to be. Too many obstacles.

I put Albania out of my mind and embraced reality. Here, there are plenty of restaurants and bars with delicious coffee and soft, cream-filled cornetti. I walked toward the water and made my way across the entrance to a marina and along the shoreline. Ahead was a graceful curve that research had told me could be the Via Traiana route that took the Roman poet Horace and his fellow diplomats "even to the very walls of Barium that abounds in fish."

This spot is thought to have been occupied since 1500 B.C. When the Romans came in the late Republican era, it was considered not very important in the ancient scheme of things, despite its port and strategic location. Barium did not gain municipal status until 89 B.C. Horace, who passed through in 37 B.C., did not seem to think much of the place. His party likely stayed at an inn somewhere near where I was wandering along the coast before they moved on to Gnatia farther south. There are almost no traces of Roman ruins here.

I found only one small vestige of Roman presence. I walked a short distance to Piazza del Ferrarese, which dates to the seventeenth century. There, cordoned off on the edge of the square in front of a small restaurant, is a road section, perhaps twenty-five feet long and eight feet wide. Urban legend says this is a section of the Via Traiana, but folks I talked to discounted that. It could simply be a bit of a lesser street through the ancient town. It is too narrow to be a major Roman road, but the rest could still be hidden under the piazza's pavements.

The uncovered road is made up of two layers. The top relates to the sixteenth century when the nearby gate to the city used to be in this area. It was later destroyed. There are large hand-squared paving stones laid in a regular arrangement. Below are smaller slabs of random shapes, laid irregularly. These are not Roman, but a Roman-laid street could be below that, now well out of sight. One saving factor for the Via Traiana legend is that it is in line with the coastal roads I was looking at earlier. This lack of information fuels the speculation, aimed at tourists, that this spot is where Emperor Trajan's mighty road flowed through the tiny fish-gathering village on its way south.

I walked back to the marina area. There are two roads ahead, both in line with that small section in Piazza del Ferrarese. One, beautifully cobblestoned, heads up a slight hill and overlooks the harbor. This marina is for small craft and yachts of the wealthy; the heavily industrial port, which I had arrived at from Greece a week earlier before driving back to Brindisi, is farther to the north. The area around the marina is a bucolic spot, a delight for me to sit at a bar's table and look out over the road below. This street could have been where the Via Traiana entered the city, or perhaps it is the lower road. No one knows for sure.

I was told that there is a Roman mile marker, or *miliaria*, on the modern road below but that it was moved from its original position during Mussolini's fascist times in the 1930s and placed in a grassy spot below where I was sitting. In a line with it are recovered columns, probably medieval. At some point, I went down to the lower road and looked at the mile marker. It is certainly for the Via Traiana. Bari largely evolved into a medieval city and, unlike Brindisi, does not have much to show, on the surface at least, for its ancient past.

My host recommended, via text message, that I should meet a gentleman named Angelofabio Attolico, a Bari resident who has studied ancient roads, particularly the Via Francigena. This is the Christian pilgrims' route that begins as far away as Britain and follows much of the Via Appia and the Via Traiana from Rome to Brindisi. There are sections of it that diverge from the older roads that often fell into disrepair after the Roman period ended.

Angelofabio agreed to meet. Our visit was a nice respite for me, since he talked in greater detail about the Via Francigena, his true passion. It developed, he said, because of the disrepair problem and because swamps that Romans had kept cleared had become swampy once again, making those roads impassable in spots.

"In medieval times, there was no central power," he said. "The Romans had been a strong central state" that could keep the road systems maintained. "In medieval times, the swamps took over" and pilgrims, working their way to Constantinople and Jerusalem, had to develop drier, safer routes. "For me," he emphasized, "this is the difference: central control versus local control."

Both roads, the Via Francigena and the Via Appia, for example, come together at Terracina. I had seen special signs in the heart of Terracina's old town denoting the route of the Via Appia as also the Via Francigena. They separated after Terracina, and the Francigena followed a parallel route through the hills to Minturno and beyond, coming back together again at Benevento. From there, it used the old track of the Via Traiana to Bari and down the coast to Brindisi. Pilgrims could stay on the road, or they could take boats from several places along the coast. "Bari became an important stop on the Francigena/Traiana route by 1087 when pilgrims stopped at several places to worship saints," Angelofabio said.

It was a pleasant hour or so. He and his organization of road walkers have tackled significant portions of the Via Francigena and the parts where the Appian Way and the Via Traiana merge. I was envious of such an undertaking. And despite being a bit older than most of the participants, such a journey with a group of route experts would be a near-the-top item on my list of things still to do.

Cannae is a quick jump north from Bari. It is less than an hour along a near-coastal road, SS116. Throughout the last couple of decades, after spending numerous trips in Italy for work or pleasure, I had never made it there and regretted it. Now, with a bit of time to spare and being so close I could almost smell the horror of the battle between the Romans and Hannibal's Carthaginians, I was finally on my way.

The coastal drive was pleasant but turning a short distance inland toward the ancient city's ruins was a surprise. Going into—and later out of—the site en route to Troia, particularly along the provincial route SP3, the drive was one of the most beautiful I have ever taken in Italy. SP3 is an appealing narrow road bordered by vast fields of grapes and groves of olives. It is a wonderfully maintained land. It took a moment to realize, as I spied high atop a ridge the edge of ruins of the village of Cannae that overlooked this land, that this plain was the battlefield, a site of extreme human destruction fought hand-to-hand, face-to-face between two mighty armies.

I was the only visitor at the museum entrance to the ruins of the ancient city. I saw only two employees and one of them, a man who seemed to be the one in charge, waved as I drove up and motioned me into a private staff parking area close to the entrance. "Not many visitors today," he said. "You can park here." I got a ticket, walked up a short hillside, and entered the ruins through an ancient gate. The age of this town's founding is hard to determine but, according to historian Michael Grant, "discoveries on and around the site go back to prehistoric times." He adds the town at the time of the battle, in 216 B.C., was "a small fortress and an important supply base" for the Romans. There is a river nearby, then known as the Aufidus (modern Ofanto). The battle was fought downstream from the town, and there is some debate over whether it took place on the right or left bank. The river has changed course several times over two millennia.

I walked the length of the Roman street, almost too eager to get to the promontory. What caught my attention as I hurried along were stone signposts at the ends of each cross street. The streets were named. I could not remember seeing signs carved in stone like this in the many other ruins I have wandered in over the years. A nice touch I remember thinking. Conveniently for me there was a comfortable bench at the promontory's tip overlooking the road below on which I had entered this bountiful plain. The way the land, sprawling as far as the eye could see, was laid out seemed to me—a native of Idaho who grew up in beautiful farming country—masterful.

I did not need to know the logistics of the battle or the layout of the armies of the two sides as they faced each other that August day. I did know the Romans had a superior force, perhaps eighty thousand soldiers and calvary. Hannibal had forty thousand infantry and ten thousand calvary. Hannibal's edge was the heavy sirocco winds, warm winds carrying North African sand. He positioned his army so that the Romans, commanded by two inexperienced consuls and facing him, had the stinging sand in their faces. That impediment, plus ingenious tactical maneuvers, almost completely wiped out the Romans. Only a few escaped to nearby towns.

The numbers of those killed vary. Different ancient historians give differing estimates. Livy gives the number at fifty-five thousand; Polybius says seventy thousand. Of course, there were Carthaginian losses as well. Livy says eight thousand. Polybius reports fifty-seven hundred.

This is the way Polybius describes the aftermath:

> The result of this battle, such as I have described it, had the consequences which both sides expected. For the Carthaginians by their victory were thenceforth masters of nearly the whole of the Italian coast which is called Magna Graecia. Thus the Tarentines immediately submitted; and the Arpani and some of the Campanian states invited Hannibal to come to them; and the rest were with one consent turning their eyes to the Carthag-

inians: who, accordingly, began now to have high hopes of being able to carry even Rome itself by assault. On their side the Romans, even after this disaster, despaired of retaining their supremacy over the Italians, and were in the greatest alarm, believing their own lives and the existence of their city to be in danger, and every moment expecting that Hannibal would be upon them.

Of course, we know that Hannibal decided against attacking Rome. He enjoyed his successes for a few more years, promising, as I mentioned in an earlier chapter, the citizens of Capua that their tiny village would become the new Rome. Four years after Cannae, for example, he captured and destroyed the village of Heraclea, whose ruins near Troia I would visit in a few days. But his fortunes began to falter, and by 203 B.C. he was pinned against the Ionian shoreline at Capo Colonna, near Crotone, along the sole of the Italian boot, hastily loading the Carthaginians in his army onto boats and leaving for Carthage across the Ionian Sea and the Strait of Sicily. There, the pursuing Romans would engage him one last time and crush Carthage. Ultimately, he had failed to overtake a powerful republic, and the Mediterranean remained, for several hundred more years, under Roman control.

I still have time to make the easy drive from Cannae to my two-day stop in Troia, a seventy-five-mile trip along a rural route through lovely countryside that got me closer, at some point, to getting back onto the Via Traiana. This was a bit south of the slightly faster route through Foggia, a large city I wanted to avoid. A critical connecting point on the route I chose is the town of Ascoli Satriano, which I knew was on the

Via Traiana. The town displays two Traiana milestones just a few feet apart on a street corner in the middle of the old town. I would visit them the next day. I at least knew I was following the ancient route between Ascoli and Troia, just twenty miles away. The road passes through each village. It flows around the foot of the hill that Ascoli dominates and then plows directly through the middle of Troia, serving as its beautifully cobblestoned main street.

It was late when I arrived in Troia. I settled in and wandered around the old town center looking for dinner, knowing I was walking just a few feet above the Via Traiana, preserved beneath cobblestones. I found food at a delightful *ristorante* and made it my base for the next two days. I was looking forward to the morning. I was scheduled to meet Nico Moscatelli, who was driving over from Foggia. Angelofabio Attolico in Bari had recommended him. Nico, an authority on the ruins at nearby Herdonia, agreed to show them to me. He also assured me that the Via Traiana, built three centuries after Hannibal destroyed the place in 210 B.C., ran through the middle of those ruins.

We met on the Via Traiana—its modern name is Via Regina Margherita—in front of the Troia cathedral about midmorning. Nico is an affable man who lightly wears his extensive learning and immediately comes across as someone who could be a best friend. We drove to Herdonia along an interesting rural provincial route, SP110, past fallow fields prepping for spring. The small modern village of Ordona, which took over one of Herdonia's ancient names, was close by. I was surprised when we turned down a private lane and stopped in front of an obviously lived-in farmhouse, complete with a couple of barking but friendly dogs.

"What is left of Herdonia is on private land, owned by the gentleman who lives here," Nico said as we walked around the side of the home and a short distance beyond. "I know him well, and we have permission to be here."

The ruins were only discovered after World War II and have been partially uncovered. There is no gate or ticket booth or any employees whatsoever. Because the land is private and there is no real parking area, I assume visitors must have guides who have made arrangements with the farmer. Nico, to my knowledge, is not only a tour guide but also a scholar of archaeology. He comes and goes as he pleases.

The stones, piled in appropriate stacks denoting baths, temples, and homes, are below our sight level as we walk along. Then, we turn slightly to the left and they leap out at us, arrayed across a wide space: straight ahead and left and right. We must drop down into an array of stones arranged like a wide pathway. We clamber down a bank into the shallow bowl below and land on well-aligned stones. This, Nico said, is the ancient Via Traiana. Now uncovered for only a few hundred feet in the ruins, it leads us into the area that once was a Roman forum. There, it makes a sharp right—unusual for a Roman road. Normally they turn on a wide curve. Not here. The road runs for several feet and then disappears into a high dirt bank that marks a boundary of one side of Herdonia's uncovered remains. Both ends of the road, where it disappears under several feet of earth, point their way across farmers' fields, primed to grow a lot of juicy Italian tomatoes, wheat, and olive groves with trees two hundred years old, not to reveal itself again for miles beyond.

In ancient times, Herdonia was spread over three hills encircled by a defensive wall a mile and a quarter long. The remains of its defensive walls attest to what must have been a series of battles over several centuries with various invaders. One of them was Hannibal, who took over the city after his 216 B.C. victory at Cannae, and many of the town's elites pledged their support as he led his army through the Apulian campaign. The Romans retook it in 212, and Hannibal roared back in 210, killing thirty-one thousand Romans and their allies over a period of two weeks. The result for Herdonia? It was razed and then burned and its population was transported farther south to the village of Metapontum.

Those left behind made do with what they could in the ruins, rebuilding here and there in later years. What eventually revived the city was the construction of the Via Traiana, and it was able to flourish once again at its key spot on the commercially important road. Already by the end of the fourth century, the forum appeared to be unused and occupied by chapels and necropolises. The final destruction of the city occurred within the Gothic War in the sixth century. Eventually, in the ninth century, focus shifted to a hillock to the north where a three-aisled church was later transformed into a castle that was inhabited until the fifteenth century. There are few traces left. In the seventeenth century, life shifted to the present town of Ordona, beginning as a rural residence for Jesuits.

Nico and I wander across a wide, open area to a mound of earth marking another boundary. There, snuggled against a stone wall, was the remaining floor area of what Nico said was a temple, one of the most important and ancient, to my old deity, the goddess Diana. Not much remains of what honored her. There are walls nearby that show the colored stones and hatch-mark placement of stones I have seen in numerous Roman ruins. And there, with a view from Diana's stone floor, are walls two and three feet high, denoting the remains of stores (*tabernae*) and houses. They are scattered over a wide area, almost hidden by wild grass. In Herdonia, archaeologists have much work ahead. Money and time, given the number of ruins scattered throughout Puglia, are scarce.

My time in Troia is running out. I walked the extent of the old town the day after Nico's visit. Its origins are trapped in the dark mists of time. Different spots are said to have held small settlements around this hillside. The town I am visiting is purely a medieval creation that dates to only 1019. Legend says that the Greek hero Diomedes, who participated in the destruction of Troy, founded the city. Some called it Aecae, but the name Troia apparently stuck over the passage of time. Medievalists, during the Byzantine Empire, only point to the 1019 date as its founding. I saw the plaque in Latin that had been placed in 1127 on the right side of the Troia cathedral.

I had a moment of cultural pleasure during my two early morning walks on those cobblestones. As I rested on the cathedral steps, I watched parents driving up to the courtyard of a medieval building directly across the way. Tiny bundles of uniformed elementary students climbed out of the cars and eagerly trotted up the steps and through the doorway of what obviously is a local school. Teachers, identically dressed in heavy long blue dresses fronted in white, greeted the children, calling out their names and recognizing them one by one. It was a nice moment experiencing a truly cultural event. All of the parents would wait in their cars until their offspring were inside this massive, beautiful old building, and then they'd drive off to begin their days.

My goal during the second day was to tour the countryside and spend some time in Ascoli Satriano. It is close by, and Nico had recommended the visit because of the town's display of two Via Traiana mile markers. A few feet apart, they do not represent any legitimate placement along the Traiana. They come from the area between Troia (ancient Aecae) and Herdonia. The road does not run through the middle of the town like it does at Troia. It sweeps around the base of the hill and now is covered in pavement by a series of local roads.

I found a reference that the Irish writer James Joyce mentioned Ascoli Satriano in his massive undertaking *Ulysses*. I looked everywhere I could to see what he said about the town, but no reference material seemed to know. My only solution would be to read the book, an undertaking I would have to put off for some time to come.

I did find out that an earthquake destroyed this delightful small town in 1456. But it was rebuilt. It is a survivor. The Romans, in the third century B.C., destroyed it and brutally executed its combatants. The Saracens razed the town in the ninth century, and it rebelled against the Byzantines in the eleventh century. It seems always to recover from adversity.

The museum there is worth a visit with its remarkable displays of carved marbles, including the two griffins of Ascoli Satriano. This was a dramatic sight. I understood, speaking my basic Italian with the woman guarding the room, that grave robbers from Foggia, in the mid-1970s in an area of the town uncovered these beautifully carved creatures, identical and facing each other in a well-lit display. The griffins were part of a collection of twenty-three marbles found in a fourth century B.C. tomb. These creatures, two winged griffins with the heads of dragons and the bodies of lions that were tearing apart a fawn, mysteriously ended up in the J. Paul Getty Museum in Los Angeles along with two other marble pieces purloined from the tomb. I remembered seeing the griffins several years earlier in a visit to that famed museum. A court battle ensued. In 2007, the three pieces were returned to their rightful place in the small museum in Ascoli Satriano. I spent a long time in that museum, looking at all the marbles and revisiting the griffins. Such magnificent art from so long ago.

When I left, I had one other place to find. I had heard there was a Roman bridge in the area that was still being used. It is along a narrow country road and carries farm equipment and local traffic. I got directions and put them, step by step, into my car's navigator and found it. It has two arches and is built of stone in typical Roman fashion. The river is not wide at this spot. While I was there, a handful of farm trucks passed by and went over the bridge.

I erroneously believed that it carried the Via Traiana. The provincial country road is on SP105, and the bridge spans the Carapelle river. I sent a message to Nico, asking if it is a Traiana bridge. No. He said it is a bridge on the ancient Via Eclanensis, sometimes called the Via Herdonitana. Trajan had it built to feed traffic onto the Via Traiana. This road and bridge get almost no mention in the research I did.

I returned to Troia in the late afternoon, had dinner at my favorite restaurant, and prepared for my longer drive the next day to Benevento. This move to the heart of a major city would be a sharp contrast to the quiet rural life I had been experiencing.

Benevento is a modern city with little to remind us of its ancient past. The Arch of Trajan, of course, is a centerpiece. It was built where the Via Appia entered the city and was the starting point for the emperor's new road eastward to the coast before turning south toward Brundisium. I had just followed its modern equivalent into the city from Troia. The Via Appia, which I followed two months earlier from near here, went on to head more directly south, reaching Taranto and then shifting eastward to Brindisi.

It is hard to know where the pathways for these roads are through modern Benevento. I stayed for two nights at a place on Viale Antonio Mellusi, which could have been the Via Appia route southward. A walking guide I later discovered warns the traveler that once the route leaves the city proper, it eventually joins the treacherous-for-walkers SS7, the Via Appia Nuova, south of the city.

Like in Bari, not much appears on the surface of the modern Benevento that relates to the Roman town. In addition to the grand arch, no longer a part of the city's long-ago removed defensive wall, there are the nicely walkable Ponte Leproso over the Sabato River that I had visited earlier in my journey and the functional ruins of a Roman theater. I stayed briefly in the city, anxious to have enough time to better explore the coast just north of Naples and southwest of the Via Appia route through ancient Capua. My only full day in Benevento involved a long walk along my street to the Arch of Trajan and then a stroll through the walkable center.

Benevento has a very old prehistory. Again, we encounter Diomedes, the Greek hero who was credited with the founding of Troia. This, of course, like for Troia, is a mythical tradition. Credit for the town's origins is likely given to a people known as the Osci and then later it became a settlement of the Samnites—the two groups shared the Oscan language—and gave the village the name Malies, which later led to Maloenton, and eventually the name Maleventum. These names, apparently from the early Greek, seem to refer to herds of sheep or goats. When viewed in Latin, it insinuates "bad luck."

Rome entered the picture as it fought a series of wars against the Samnites. After a number of back-and-forth wins and losses, it finally defeated all the Samnite peoples by 290 B.C. In 268 B.C., the Romans changed the name to Beneventum, with a meaning more along the lines of "good luck." It became a Roman municipality in 86 B.C. By the fourth century A.D., Beneventum was second only to Capua as the most populous city in the south.

I spent a couple of hours sitting on a bench near the front of Trajan's arch. Its still-sharp carvings on the structure's marble coverings that were quarried from a Greek island are impressive. Of course, it has been restored extensively over the millennia, in the seventeenth, eighteenth, and nineteenth centuries. There have been earthquakes that threatened to topple it and, of course, weathering is an issue.

The carvings represent a wide variety of activities involving Emperor Trajan. He is shown being greeted by the three deities associated with the Capitoline Hill in Rome, in his involvement with other structures in that capital city, and being honored for victory over Dacia. That campaign also is the subject of his column that still stands in Rome next to his market. Other panels depict Trajan in Beneventum and the sacrifices associated with the opening of the Via Traiana. There is much more represented, of course, on this work of the classical world created by anonymous craftsmen. It was hard to pull away. The modern city buzzes around it. Thankfully, the arch is cordoned off, and the road that once passed under it has long since been diverted around it, much like the road under the Arch of Constantine in Rome.

The next morning, as I was preparing to leave Benevento and head southwest to the Gulf of Naples for my final explorations close to but not directly on the Via Appia, I drove back down toward the arch and miraculously found a free parking spot just a few feet away. I walked around the arch one last time, savoring the marble carvings and weaving in and out of its early morning shadows. I returned to the bench where I had spent those few hours the day before and leafed through several notes I had accumulated.

Trajan was one of the more enlightened emperors, a lucky thirteenth and the first of the second century A.D. Born in Spain, he transformed much of the Roman world, launched numerous building projects, and oversaw an empire that grew to its largest size under his leadership. When he died, in A.D. 117, Rome had lost much of Mesopotamia, but its frontiers remained relatively stable for a few more centuries.

I returned to Santa Maria Capua Vetere and dropped down toward Naples, but I stopped just a few miles short of entering that remarkable city. I only had time to visit its bay, where ancient folks—foreign armies, Roman legions, praetors, proconsuls, and a handful of Christianity's earliest apostles—landed at the port of Puteoli (modern Pozzuoli) and trudged on to Rome—the rich in carts, others on the backs of mules, but most on foot. I also wanted to see Baia, known in the classical period as Baiae when it was a playground for the Roman elite.

One of those on foot—and possibly in chains—was Saint Paul. He had been traveling around the Mediterranean preaching, baptizing, and founding congregations. Actual churches would come later. Before arriving on the Italian Peninsula, Paul and his fellow travelers had gone to Malta, because they were shipwrecked off the coast there during a storm, then to Siracusa in Sicily. When their new ship landed in Puteoli after a brief visit to Rhegium (modern Reggio di Calabria) in A.D. 58, Paul and his party spent a week with fellow believers. Through all this, he was under Roman guard, soldiers who were assigned to lead the apostle to Rome. There, he was to be judged by Emperor Nero, who was not at all disposed to Paul's new religion.

Accounts differ, but eventually the Romans led Paul and his group inland from Puteoli to either ancient Capua or along a rough coastal pathway that became, thirty-eight years later, the Via Domitiana (today's modern highway called Via Domiziana). If they went this way, which is likely, they would quickly arrive at Sinuessa, now only a handful of ruins in the modern city of Mondragone.

Either way, the group would have joined the Via Appia, following it all the way to Rome, more than one hundred miles away. There Paul lived not in a prison but rather in a house for at least two years, visiting fellow Christians, writing letters that were incorporated into the New Testament, and continuing to preach and convert. Eventually, this freedom ended; Nero imprisoned him and had him executed at some point in the midsixties of the first century A.D.

To make a journey to Pozzuoli and Baia, and after signing in to my lodgings in Bacoli, I made a quick stop at the ruins of ancient Cumae. My guide was Arianna Castiglia from Bacoli, a small town with ties in antiquity and located close to those other cities. "Cumae was the origin of everything," she told me. It was the Greeks' first mainland settlement in Italy, giving birth, from the eighth to the fifth century B.C., to a collection of cities and villages throughout Southern Italy and Sicily. The Romans called this Magna Graecia, or Greater Greece. My friend the historian Lou Mendola prefers the Greek expression Megálē Hellás.

"Megálē Hellás was the entire Grecophone part of Italy south of Rome," he said. I have often surmised that there are more Greek ruins in Southern Italy and Sicily than there are in Greece. That may not be true as I have not extensively traveled through Greece, but it is a good guess.

Cumae is twelve miles west of Naples in a land known as the Phlegraean Fields. There was once, forty thousand years ago, a great volcanic explosion that created this wide caldera. Twenty-four smaller craters, volcanic edifices, and vents all sit inside it. Lakes occupy a few of the craters, lakes that the Roman elite enjoyed during long respites from life in their cluttered, smelly capital city. But the land still rumbles and tumbles, slips and slides due to volcanic activity far underground. It also is referred to as Campi Flegrei, or the "fiery fields."

There is always the threat of earthquakes here. The late William Murray, a writer for *The New Yorker* magazine, described it best, in his book *The Last Italian*:

> Directly under [Pozzuoli], about a mile and a half beneath the surface, is a huge lake of volcanic magma. When it heats up, it exerts an upward pressure that causes the ground to rise; when it cools, the surface sinks. "It's as if the city were perched on the chest of a sleeping giant," was the way it was explained to me by one of the scientists at the local [bradyseism] research center. . . . "A single cough and it would be destroyed."

Murray taught me a new word. "Bradyseism" is defined as "a gradual rise or fall in the earth's crust."

During my three days traveling around that fiery field, I did not feel any tremors. With everything calm underfoot, I could revisit Cumae with Arianna without any concern. This was my second time there. I had visited Cumae many years earlier as part of a small group tour and vividly remember an experience we had at the cave of the Cumaean Sybil. We were led to the spot where our then guide said the Sybil gave out words of wisdom, advice, and predictions. Mythology tells us that as a young woman the Sybil had asked Apollo for eternal life. He granted it. But her great mistake was that she did not ask for eternal youth. She aged, became decrepit and got smaller and smaller. The Cumaeans were disrespectful and placed her in a hanging basket. Eventually, all that remained was her voice.

Now, Arianna said, there are those who believe that this was not her cave at all but rather a Roman crypt. When I was there several years ago, no one mentioned the crypt idea. Then, in what our guide said was the Sybil's chamber, a Stanford University classics professor read an excerpt to us from the *Aeneid*. It was charming. We heard such well-crafted words, written two thousand years ago, spoken in such a setting where its author, Virgil, likely had visited.

Climbing around the ruins led me to a final meeting with one of my favorite goddesses, whose path I had crossed several times during this three-month trip. There, on a high spot with a clear view of the Tyrrhenian Sea two thousand feet away— the sea in ancient times had lapped at the base of these pagan grounds—was the Temple of Diana. Arianna told me that archaeologists had studied its shape and computed astronomical positions that would have been present in ancient times. They discovered that from the spot where the goddess's statue stood at the back of the temple floor, it was possible that one could observe the full moon rising on August 13 in 21 B.C.

After all, the Ides of August (the thirteenth), as I had learned during my visit two months earlier to her temple at Nemi, is the date for her annual festival. So she, to the Romans, was the goddess of the moon, among many other responsibilities. This temple at Cumae was built around this time near the end of the republic. Because a temple to Diana's brother Apollo was nearby, the pair made a perfect connection between the sun and the moon. Apollo has always been associated with the sun since he took that job over from the long-forgotten titan Helios. As was their usual practice to negate pagan influences, Christians, in the fifth century A.D., built a church on Apollo's temple site. Nothing much remains of that either.

Arianna and I moved on, passing through modern Pozzuoli. There, she took me to a small, narrow cobblestone road, the modern Via Celle, which she believes was the route travelers landing at the port took to join the Via Appia, a short distance to the north and their pathway to Rome. The road, just wide enough for one vehicle at a time, runs for less than a mile and passes burial places—some more recent, others pagan—and is bordered at several points with remains of Roman walls. There is a restaurant along the route where workers once found the remains of an early Christian home. Here, as in many spots in Italy, the modern crisscrosses with the distant past. A Roman tomb sits in a tranquil spot along a dirt path through an orchard.

We find ourselves traveling through a tall arch nearly sixty-seven feet high and almost twenty feet wide that seems to hold together two high mountains. It is an artificial cut in a high mountain ridge ordered by the emperor Domitian in A.D. 95 as part of his project to build the Via Domitiana. That is the road that ultimately tied Naples to the Via Appia, along the earlier coastline route to Sinuessa.

My trip is winding down. In a few days I will be at Lake Nemi for a short return visit and then to Rome for my journey home. But for now, Arianna takes me to Baia, the modern name for Baiae, which was the pleasure zone for Roman elite. Volcanic vents beneath the city provided copious supplies of hot water for several baths, one of the great draws for Romans. Just a few miles from Cumae, this was where Julius Caesar, Nero, and long lines of emperors and the wealthy had magnificent villas, ruins of which line the hillside above the bay. Nearby, ancient Bauli (today's Bacoli) also had its share of villas and baths.

The ruins in the adjacent towns are extensive. Augustus turned the area into an imperial property; the emperor Hadrian died in Caesar's villa in 138. But Baiae's glorious end was nigh. Muslim raiders sacked the city and probably much of the surrounding area several hundred years later, and in the fifteen hundreds, the volcanic vents that provided such hot-water pleasure to the pleasure-seekers turned on the people, and more than three hundred feet of the seafront slowly slipped into the shallow bay. Now, glass-bottom boats ply the bay for curious tourists interested in viewing remains of structures and mosaics in the shallow waters.

The next day, my last before heading north, my host, Gennaro Opera, put me on the back of his motorcycle and took me around the area for a final grand tour. It was a remarkable, high-speed journey, once again through the fiery fields and to the northern outskirts of Naples. The region is compact, easily accessible, and well worth the journey. But I was not quite finished. Later, Gennaro's daughter, Anna Opera, took me to one last site to visit—the Piscina Mirabilis (wondrous pool). There I was met by Gino Pezzullo, my guide for a quick tour of one of the Roman world's largest cisterns. This is in what was part of Bauli at a point near the bay where the imperial Roman fleet was based.

Gino ticks off the impressive numbers: the cistern is 49 feet high, 236 feet long, and 82 feet wide. The ceiling is held in place by 48 pillars. We enter and climb down modern stairs; the ancient steps would be too treacherous. The interior took my breath away. I could just imagine what this massive cathedral of water storage would have looked like. The piscina would occasionally be drained to allow toilers to scrape the floor, deep in mud that had accumulated over time as soil, mixed in with water, slowly filtered downward.

Originally, it was thought that the purpose of the mammoth structure, ordered by Augustus to be built, was to provide fresh drinking water for crews of the Roman ships that often went on long cruises around the Mediterranean. But Gino said later thinking disputes this. The aqueduct that supplied the piscina was extended to carry water directly to the ships at Portus Julius. More likely, a structure like a giant cistern, built at huge expense, was to serve the villas built by the wealthy Romans.

Gino and I walked back up those sturdy stairs and into to late fall sunlight. We said our goodbyes. Once again, I am overwhelmed by Roman ingenuity from so long, long ago. Of course, things can be built more quickly and for less money when slave labor—captured during interminable wars raging around the vast Mediterranean—is available. But we also must give credit to the Roman engineering prowess that created cities with massive temples, forums, basilicas, coliseums, theaters, and triumphal arches that knew no equal in the ancient world.

I got my first taste of this by learning how they built the roads that were the envy of all who traveled on them, getting their sandaled feet, the wheels of mule-pulled carts, and horses' hooves out of the mud of protohistoric Italy and then, high and dry, through the four of five countries seen during my long trip.

Years of traveling in Italy suggest that I can only lightly brush against it all.

SELECTED BIBLIOGRAPHY

Alio, Jacqueline, and Louis Mendola. *Kingdom of Sicily 1130–1266: The Norman-Swabian Age and the Identity of a People*. New York: Trinacria Editions, 2022.

Ashby, Thomas, and Robert Gardner. "The Via Traiana." *Papers of the British School at Rome*, Vol. 8, No. 5, 104–171 (1916).

Baños, José Miguel. "The Brutal Beheading of Cicero, Last Defender of the Roman Republic." *National Geographic* (May 24, 2021).

Beard, Mary. *SPQR: A History of Ancient Rome*. New York: Liveright, 2015.

Brunwasser, Matthew. "Letter from Albania: A Road Trip Through Time." *Archaeology*, January/February 54–64 (2018).

Caesar, Julius. *Civil War II*. Edited and translated by Cynthia Damon. Cambridge: Harvard University Press, 2016.

Canter, H. V. "Venusia and the Native Country of Horace." *The Classical Journal*, Vol. 26, no. 6 (March 1931).

Chiarelli, Leonard C. *A History of Muslim Sicily*. Second revised edition. Sta Venera, Malta: Midsea Books, 2018.

Ehrman, Bart D. *The Triumph of Christianity: How a Forbidden Religion Swept the World*. New York: Simon & Schuster, 2018.

Everitt, Anthony. *Augustus: The Life of Rome's First Emperor*. New York: Random House, 2006.

Forbes, Urquhart A., and Arnold C. Burmester. *Our Roman Highways*. London: F. E. Robinson and Co., 1904.

Franz, Gordon. "'How Beautiful Are the Feet' on the Via Egnatia." *Bible and Spade*, Vol. 27, no. 2, 36–45 (2014).

Frazzetta, Andrea. "A Roman Era 'Superhighway' Is Disappearing. Italy Has a Plan to Save It." *National Geographic* (June 2, 2022).

Freeman, Philip. *Julius Caesar*. New York: Simon & Schuster Paperbacks, 2008.

Garilli, Erika, Frederico Autelitano, and Felice Giuliani. "A Study for the Understanding of the Roman Pavement Design Criteria." *Journal of Cultural Heritage* 25: 87–93 (2017).

Giustozzi, Nunzio. *The Appian Way: Guide*. Milan: Mondadori Electa S.p.A., 2014.

Goethe, Johann Wolfgang von. *Italian Journeys: 1786–1788*. New York: Penguin Classics, 1992.

Goldsworthy, Adrian. *Caesar: Life of a Colossus*. New Haven: Yale University Press, 2006.

Grant, Michael. *A Guide to the Ancient World: A Dictionary of Classical Place Names*. New York: Barnes & Noble Books, 1986.

Hickman, Kennedy. "Wars of the Second Triumvirate: Battle of Philippi." ThoughtCo, February 16, 2021, thoughtco.com/second-triumvirate-battle -of-philippi-2360881.

Hoare, Sir Richard Colt. *A Classical Tour Through Italy and Sicily*. Cambridge: Cambridge University Press, 2015.

Holland, James. *Italy's Sorrow: A Year of War, 1944–1945*. New York: St. Martin's Press, 2008.

Holland, Tom. *Rubicon: The Last Years of the Roman Republic*. New York: Doubleday, 2003.

Hughes, Bettany. *Istanbul: A Tale of Three Cities*. Boston: Da Capo Press, 2017.

Jensen, Erik. "The Road to Peace: Horace's Fifth Satire as Travel Literature." *World History Connected*, February 2013, https://worldhistoryconnected .press.uillinois.edu/10.1/forum_jensen.html.

Kassabova, Kapka. *To the Lake: A Balkan Journey of War and Peace*. Minneapolis: Greywolf Press, 2020.

Killgrove, Christina. "DNA Study Pinpoints When the Ancient Greeks Colonized Sicily and Italy." *Forbes*, July 23, 2015.

Kline, A. S. *Horace: The Satires*. Retrieved May 3, 2022, from https://www .poetryintranslation.com/PITBR/Latin/HoraceSatiresBkISatI.php (2005).

Kreutz, Barbara M. *Before the Normans: Southern Italy in the Ninth and Tenth Centuries*. Philadelphia: University of Pennsylvania Press, 1991.

Langguth, A. J. *A Noise of War: Caesar, Pompey, Octavian and the Struggle for Rome*. New York: Simon & Schuster, 1994.

Latium Mirabile. "Appia Antica in Itri." Atlas Obscura, https://www.atlasobscura.com/places/appia-antica-in-itri (June 5, 2020).

Livy. *The War with Hannibal*. Translated by Aubrey de Sélincourt. London: Penguin Books, 1972.

Magli, Giulio, Eugenio Realini, Mirko Reguzzoni, and Daniele Sampietro. "Uncovering a Masterpiece of Roman Engineering: The Project of Via Appia Between Colle Pardo and Terracina." *Journal of Cultural Heritage* 15: 665–69 (2014).

Murray, William. *The Last Italian: Portrait of a People*. New York: Prentice Hall Press, 1991.

Musurillo, Herbert A. "Horace's Journey to Brundisium: Fact or Fiction?" *The Classical Weekly*, Vol. 48, no. 12, April 18, 159–62. Baltimore: Johns Hopkins University Press, 1955.

Norwich, John Julius. *Absolute Monarchs: A History of the Papacy*. New York: Random House, 2011.

O'Sullivan, Firmin. *The Egnatian Way*. Harrisburg, Pa.: Stackpole Books, 1972.

Piperno, Roberto. "Minturnae." www.romeartlover.it, February 2018.

Poetry Foundation. "Horace: 65 B.C.–8 B.C." poetryfoundation.org/poets/Horace.

Polybius. "The Battle of Cannae, 216 BCE." *Ancient History Sourcebook*. Translated by Evelyn S. Shuckburgh. New York: Fordham University, 1998.

Shakespeare, William. *Julius Caesar*. Mineola, N.Y.: Dover Publications, 2009.

Stenhouse, Margaret. *The Goddess of the Lake: Origins of a Myth and the Roman Ships of Nemi*. Frascati: Poligraphica Laziale s.r.l, Italyupdate.it—revised and updated (2016).

Stillwell, Richard, William L. MacDonald, and Marian Holland McAllister. *The Princeton Encyclopedia of Classical Sites*. Princeton: Princeton University Press, 1976.

Strabo. *Strabo Geography*. Translated by Horace Leonard Jones. Cambridge: Loeb Classical Library, Harvard University Press, 1917–1924.

Strauss, Barry. *The War That Made the Roman Empire: Antony, Cleopatra, and Octavian at Actium*. New York: Simon & Schuster, 2022.

Suetonius (C. Suetonius Tranquillus). *The Twelve Caesars*. Translated by Alexander Thomson, M.D. Revised and corrected by T. Forester, Esq., A.M. Scotts Valley, Calif.: CreateSpace Independent Publishing Platform, 2013.

Swinburne, Henry. *Travels in the Two Sicilies*. Miami: HardPress, 2017.

Tacitus, Publius Cornelius. *The Annals*. Translated by Alfred John Church and William Jackson Brodribb. Rome101.com.

Thompson, Logan. "Roman Roads." *History Today Ltd.,* Vol. 47, no. 2 (1997).

Tsatsopoulou-Kaloudi, Polyxeni. *Via Egnatia: History and the Route Through Thrace*. Translated by Freya Evenson. Athens: Ministry of Culture, Education, and Religious Affairs Archaeological Receipts Fund, 2015.

Van Attekum, Marietta, and Holger de Bruin. *Via Egnatia on Foot: A Journey Into History*. Driebergen, Holland: Via Egnatia Foundation, 2017.

Vergano, Dan. "Grapes Domesticated 8,000 Years Ago." *USA Today*, January 19, 2011.

Vermaseren, Maartin Jozef. *Mithriaca I: The Mithraeum at S. Maria Capua Vetere*. Leiden: E. J. Brill, 1971.

Von Hagen, Victor W. *The Roads That Led to Rome*. Cleveland and New York: World Publishing Company, 1967.

INDEX